NTC's Language Project Books

Weit und breit 1

National Textbook Company
a division of NTC/Contemporary Publishing Group, Inc.
Lincolnwood, Illinois USA

Development and Production: Elm Street Publications, Wellesley, MA
Composition: Jan Ewing, Ewing Systems, New York, NY
Illustrations: Len Shalansky
Electronic Art: William J. Cataldi, Ewing Systems, NY

ISBN: 0-658-00312-7 (hardbound)
ISBN: 0-658-00098-5 (softbound)

Published by National Textbook Company,
a division of NTC/Contemporary Publishing Group, Inc.
4255 West Touhy Avenue
Lincolnwood (Chicago), Illinois 60646-1975 U.S.A.

Manufactured in the United States of America.

99 00 01 02 03 04 05 QB 9 8 7 6 5 4 3 2 1

Inhalt

To the Student

You are studying a foreign language—German. And languages are meant to be spoken. But people talk for a reason: maybe to tell a friend about something that's just happened, or to ask about the time a movie starts. Well, ***Weit und breit 1*** also provides reasons for using language—different situations in which you need to speak, read, and write German.

Weit und breit 1 consists of ten projects that relate to topics ordinarily taught in first-year German. You may do them in the order that fits your textbook. Why projects? Because each one has a different goal and includes a different reason for using German. Because you'll have the satisfaction of actually using German to create something. Some of the projects involve:

- Setting up and going to a restaurant typical of a German-speaking area
- Planning mini-Olympic games for the German-speaking world
- Creating a German-language weather report
- Producing a German-language fashion show
- Setting up a health and fitness center for German-speaking clients
- Making a holiday calendar for the German-speaking world

You'll reach the goals of these projects in many different ways. To make a calendar, for example, you'll research holidays in German-speaking countries and regions. That research could be done on the World Wide Web, if you have access to it. Once on the Web, you can search for information in both German and English! To give a weather report, you'll need to change Fahrenheit temperatures into Celsius because after all, that's what people in the German-speaking countries use and understand.

A resource section of special tools is available in the Almanac in the back of ***Weit und breit 1***. It contains lots of helpful information, including the following:

- A list of the German-speaking countries with their capitals and a monetary unit chart with directions for changing money from dollars to the currencies of various German-speaking countries

- A guide for doing searches on the World Wide Web
- Extra vocabulary related to the projects you're working on
- A metric chart with directions for converting standard U.S. measurements

Weit und breit 1 includes other features to help you. Each project begins with a list of the tasks to be performed. This is a kind of road map showing what you can accomplish. There is even a **Verknüpfungen** (*Connections*) box indicating other subject areas related to this project, such as history, art, technology, or study skills. The **Brauchbares** (*Useful tools*) boxes suggest sources for finding information you will need, as well as materials required for each step in the project. This may include worksheets to help you organize and present information. Worksheets are available from your teacher, and activities that use them have a worksheet icon in the margin of the text. The **Nützliche Vokabeln** (*Vocabulary*) boxes include German words and phrases you may need to complete a step in the project.

While you're working through a project, you'll see interesting tidbits of information about German-speaking countries in the **Hast du das gewusst?** (*Did you know that?*) boxes. They present interesting facts, such as which German-speaking country has won the most Olympic medals per capita in the world and how Germans cope without closets in the bedroom.

During a project, you will often work with partners or a small group of other students. In Project 6, **Das ist unsere Schule**, you might make classroom signs, or perhaps videotape important areas of the school for a student guidebook. Occasionally you'll work on your own. You may see an icon indicating that a task can be done as homework.

While you work with other students on these projects, you will have many opportunities to speak, read, and write German. You may play the role of an exchange student, talk with your host, and later write a thank-you note in German. In Project 4, you will play a game that a group has invented. You may have to read and answer questions in German.

But what if you'd like to add something extra to a project? Maybe you'd like a challenge. In each project, **Noch etwas dazu** (*Something* *extra*) sections provide those opportunities. You can spread your wings and push your German to its limits.

In these projects, German is everywhere; it is necessary and useful. You and your classmates will have the satisfaction of using German in real-life situations and enjoying it.

Viel Spaß!

PROJECT

1

Lernen wir einander kennen!

For this project, your class will plan a visit to a German-speaking country. You will be working in one of two groups. One group will consist of students from the U.S. who are "visiting" a major city in a German-speaking country. The other group will be the host students. During the course of this project, you will:

- Decide on a city in a German-speaking country to visit
- Write a letter of introduction to one of the new students you're going to meet
- Find the best flight times and fares to your destination (visitors)
- Find ways to pick up your guests at the airport and create a welcome banner (hosts)
- Introduce yourself personally to the new students
- Investigate a site for a group excursion and design postcards from the site
- Write a note to a new friend

Gute Reise!

Verknüpfungen

As you explore a new city and meet new people, you'll sharpen your skills in many areas.

- ✔ Geographie
- ✔ Geschichte
- ☐ Gesundheit und Ernährung
- ✔ Kunst
- ✔ Lernmethoden
- ✔ Mathematik
- ☐ Medien
- ☐ Musik
- ☐ Naturwissenschaft
- ✔ Technik

Look for the **Verknüpfungen** boxes throughout this project.

Warm-up: Guten Tag!

Brauchbares

- A three-ring binder or folder for each student for compiling a portfolio

A. With two or three other students, create a list of words and phrases in German that you associate with greetings and introductions. Share your ideas with your class and expand your list as you listen to your classmates' ideas. How are German greetings and introductions similar to or different from greetings and introductions in the U.S.?

B. In a group of three or four, discuss what greetings and introductions in the U.S. are like. What are the typical words and phrases people say when meeting someone new? Do people shake hands? How might greetings between two friends be different from those between two business associates?

Hi!
Hey!
How are you?
How do you do?
Hello!
Howdy!
It's a pleasure to meet you.
Mornin'!
Good morning!

c. As you plan and carry out your trip, you'll be putting together a portfolio of your experiences and accomplishments. You'll need a three-ring binder. Begin your portfolio by inserting the list of words and phrases you and your classmates brainstormed. You may want to refer to this list throughout the project.

A Die Vorbereitungen

The German-speaking countries share a common language, but each has its own distinct geography, attractions, history, and culture. After researching various possibilities, your class will decide on one city to visit on your exchange trip.

Brauchbares

- World map
- World Map Worksheet 1.A, pages 1 and 2
- Colored markers
- Maps of German-speaking countries
- Encyclopedias
- Guidebooks for German-speaking countries
- Travel magazines or brochures with photographs of German-speaking cities
- TV programs about selected cities
- Portfolio
- The World Wide Web

1. Schritt

Wo spricht man Deutsch?

A. Working in a group of three or four students, see how many German-speaking countries and capitals you can name. Share your list with the class and write it on the board. Compare your list with the one in the Almanac at the back of this book.

B. Continue working in your group. Each person should have a copy of Map Worksheet 1.A, pages 1 and 2. Color all the German-speaking countries the same color and label each with its name. Consult your German textbook or the Almanac for help.

Verknüpfungen

- ☑ Geographie
- ☑ Lernmethoden
- ☑ Technik

C. In your group, choose two German-speaking countries on your map. Think of at least two things you associate with each one. Consider cities, famous people, arts, geographical landmarks, foods, climate, and so on. Record your associations on Map Worksheet 1.A, page 2, and share them with the class.

Land	*Assoziationen*
▶ Deutschland:	1. Berlin 2. Beethoven
Liechtenstein:	1. A small country situated between Austria and Switzerland 2. Postage stamps

Hast du das gewusst?

Switzerland has four national languages: **Deutsch**, **Französich**, **Italienisch**, and **Rätoromanisch**. **Deutsch** is spoken by approximately 65 percent of the population; **Französisch** by 19 percent; **Italienisch** by 10 percent, and **Rätoromanisch** by less than one percent. Since international businesses are quite numerous in Switzerland, the remaining five percent speak many other foreign languages. **Deutsch**, **Französisch**, and **Italienisch** are the main **Amtssprachen** (official languages) used in business and politics. In an attempt to prevent **Rätoromanisch** from dying out, the Swiss voted in 1996 to make it a partial **Amtssprache**.

2. Schritt Jetzt geht's los!

Your group's next step is to learn something new about a city in a German-speaking country that interests you. On a map, locate a city you'd like to visit in one of the countries you chose earlier and write its name on Map Worksheet 1.A, page 2. Use some of the resources listed in the **Brauchbares** box on page 6 to find out at least five facts about the city that you didn't already know. Record them on Map Worksheet 1.A, page 2.

Suchen wir im Web!

Look for information about a German-speaking city via the Web. Use the Reference or Travel sections of a Web guide to link to encyclopedias and national or local travel-related sites. Be sure to keep the addresses of sites that are of particular interest. Write them down or use the Bookmark feature of your navigation software. This feature is usually accessible from one of your pull-down menus. If any of the terms used here are unfamiliar to you, you can look them up in the Web Search Guide in the Almanac at the end of this book. The Web Search Guide also contains general guidelines for searching the Web.

3. Schritt Wohin geht die Reise?

In English, try to persuade the rest of the class that the city you've chosen would be the best destination for a student exchange trip!

A. With your group, prepare a brief but convincing presentation for your class—in English—about your city. Use the information you've gathered and try to include some photographs of the city from guidebooks, travel brochures, magazines, or the Web. Use Map Worksheet 1.A, page 1, to show where the country and city are located.

B. After the presentations, hold a class vote to determine which city is the class favorite. That city will be the destination of your student exchange trip! On Map Worksheet 1.A, page 1, outline the country your class has chosen in a contrasting color. Add Map Worksheet 1.A and the information that you gathered about your city to your portfolio.

4. Schritt Die zwei Gruppen

For much of the rest of this project, you will be working in one of two groups. One group will be the host students in the city you've chosen. The other group will be the exchange students visiting from the U.S.

B Ein Briefwechsel

Before the trip begins, the visitors and the hosts will want to find out something about each other. A short letter can provide a good introduction.

Brauchbares

- A self-portrait or a drawing of you and your family
- Portfolio

1. Schritt Wie stellt man sich vor?

Before you write a letter to one of the new students you're going to meet, think about how you want to introduce yourself.

A. Find a partner from your own group (host students or visiting students). In English, brainstorm a list of standard information that should be included in a letter of introduction. Then come up with a list of phrases in German that will help you express this information in your letter. Keep in mind whether you're host students or visiting students.

Standard information	*Phrases*
▶ *name:*	Ich heiße ___.
hometown:	Ich komme aus ___.

B. Share your German phrases with the class and make a list together on the board.

Verknüpfungen

☑ Kunst
☑ Lernmethoden

2. Schritt Persönliches

Make a list of the personal information you want to include in your letter, using the topics you brainstormed in the **1. Schritt**. If you're one of the host students, you'll need to invent a German-speaking identity: a name, address, and so on.

3. Schritt Die Briefe

A. Choose an exchange partner from the other group. Write a brief letter introducing yourself to your exchange partner. Include a self-portrait or a drawing of you and your family. For help with the format of a German letter, see the examples on the facing page and in the Almanac at the back of this book.

Nützliche Vokabeln

Liebe [*female name*]	*Dear [female name]*
Lieber [*male name*]	*Dear [male name]*
Viele Grüße	*Best regards*
Bis bald!	*See you soon!*
Ich habe keine Schwestern [Brüder].	*I don't have any sisters [brothers].*
Ich treibe gern Sport.	*I like to play sports.*
Ich spiele gern ___.	*I like to play [name of game/ musical instrument].*

B. Give your letter to your teacher for delivery to your exchange partner. If your exchange partner is a host, put his or her real name on the back so your teacher knows to whom to deliver it. Read the letter you've received and add it to your portfolio. If you have any problems understanding your letter, consult your teacher.

Chicago, den 21. September 2002

Lieber Martin,

ich heiße Tom. Ich bin 14 Jahre alt. Ich komme aus Chicago, Illinois. Ich habe zwei Brüder und einen Hund (wir sind alle auf dem Foto). Ich spiele gern Tennis, lese gern und gehe gern schwimmen. Bis bald!

Viele Grüße

Tom

XXX XXXXX
XXXX XXXXXXX XXXX
XXXX, XX

An
Herrn Martin Schmidt
Mommsengasse 6/15
A-5020 Salzburg
AUSTRIA

Hast du das gewusst?

Addresses in German-speaking countries are written differently than U.S. addresses. For example, you write the house number after the street name, instead of before it. An apartment number follows the house number. The letter above is going to Mr. Schmidt, who lives at number 6 Mommsengasse, apartment 15. Postal codes precede the city name. When writing from outside the country, include the international country code before the postal code: A for Austria, D for Germany, CH for Switzerland, and L for Liechtenstein.

Noch etwas dazu

Now see if you can find two people in your group (hosts or visitors) who have something in common with your exchange partner. Survey at least five classmates, sharing information from the letter you received. Be sure to make notes so you can tell your exchange partner later what you found out.

▶ *You:* Mein Brieffreund Tom hat zwei Brüder. Hast du auch zwei Brüder?

Group member 1: Nein, ich habe nur einen Bruder.

Group member 2: Ja, ich habe auch zwei Brüder!

C Die Reise

Before the exchange trip gets under way, the visitors need to make travel plans, and the hosts need to make plans to receive the visitors.

Brauchbares

- Airline flight schedules and fares to the city you've chosen
- The World Wide Web
- Portfolio
- Markers, paper, tape
- Computer with word-processing software

1. Schritt

Für die Gäste: Der Flug

This **Schritt** is for visitors. The visitors need to research flight times and fares to make sure they find the best bargains. Work with three or four other students from your group.

A. Using the airline flight schedules and fare lists, find out what flights are available from your hometown (or the nearest airport) to the city you've selected for the exchange trip. Make a list of five different possible dates and times. Include the arrival times in the German-speaking city and record the flight numbers and the names of the airlines.

B. Find out the fare for each of the flights. Use the monetary unit chart in the Almanac section of this book and exchange rates available from newspapers, banks, or the Web to list the prices in both dollars and the currency of the German-speaking country.

Verknüpfungen

- ✔ Kunst
- ✔ Lernmethoden
- ✔ Mathematik
- ✔ Technik

2. Schritt Für die Gastgeber: Herzlich willkommen!

A. This **Schritt** is for the hosts. Brainstorm ways of getting to the airport to pick up your guests. Choose the best way to go by taking a vote, and then decide what arrangements need to be made. Do you need to rent a vehicle?

B. Now make welcome banners to greet your visitors. Be creative and try to use both German and English on them. Use some of the materials suggested in the **Brauchbares** box on page 13. Keep the banners for later use.

WILLKOMMEN!

3. Schritt Wann fliegen wir?

Each visitor reports to the class in German the date, time, and fare of one of the flights his or her group has selected. The teacher writes the information on the board, and the class then decides which flight is the best choice for the whole group.

4. Schritt Dein Album

Add your list of flight times and fares as well as the group's final choice of a flight to your portfolio.

Hast du das gewusst?

In Germany, Austria, and Switzerland, many traffic intersections are equipped with cameras that record the flow of traffic. If you run a red light or commit another offense at such an intersection, your car and license plate are photographed. A few weeks later, a traffic violation fine will arrive in your mailbox.

Noch etwas dazu

Work with your partner from the other group. Together, prepare a telephone conversation in German. If you are the visitor, call your host partner. You'll need to introduce yourself, ask for your partner, and tell him or her where you're from. Then say where your group is arriving, what the flight number is, and the time and date you're coming. If you're a host, you'll need to answer the phone, greet your caller, and respond to his or her introduction. Then ask when the group will arrive and take down the information your partner gives you. You might need to ask the caller to repeat something.

Nützliche Vokabeln

Wer ist da, bitte?	*Who's calling, please?*
Hier ist [*name*].	*This is ___.*
Darf ich bitte mit [*name*] sprechen?	*May I please speak with ___?*
Wir fliegen von [*name of city*] ab.	*We're flying from ___.*
Wir kommen in [*name of city*] an.	*We're arriving in ___.*
Die Flugnummer ist [*number*].	*The flight number is ___.*
Wir kommen am [*date*] an.	*We're arriving on ___.*
Um wie viel Uhr kommt der Flug an?	*What time does the flight arrive?*
Der Flug kommt um [*time*] Uhr an.	*The flight arrives at ___.*
Geht das?	*Is that okay?*
Wir sehen uns um [*time*] Uhr am Flughafen.	*We'll see each other at the airport at ___.*

D Die Ankunft

When the visitors arrive, the hosts greet them at a gathering with the exchange coordinator (your teacher).

Brauchbares

- Adhesive name tags or index cards and tape
- Markers
- Welcome banners made in Section C
- Portfolio

1. Schritt

Ich heiße ...

At this first meeting, you're going to introduce yourself to the new students. Prepare a name tag to help your new friends learn your name. In addition to your name, add one piece of information about yourself in German that will help stimulate conversation with your new friends, such as your age, whether you have siblings or pets, or the name of an activity that you really enjoy.

Nützliche Vokabeln

Ich bin [14] Jahre alt.	*I'm [14] years old.*
Ich habe [einen Bruder/ zwei Schwestern].	*I have [a brother/ two sisters].*
Ich habe keine Geschwister.	*I have no brothers or sisters.*
Ich habe [zwei Katzen/ einen Hund/einen Goldfisch].	*I have [two cats/ a dog/a goldfish].*
Ich spiele gern [Fußball].	*I like to play [soccer].*
Ich [lese] gern.	*I like to [read].*

Verknüpfungen

- ☑ Kunst
- ☑ Lernmethoden

2. Schritt Und du?

Working with a partner from your group (host students or visiting students), write at least three questions in German that you want to ask your new friends when you meet.

3. Schritt Es freut mich!

Now it's time to meet your new friends! Don't forget to wear your name tag and bring your questions to the introductory gathering. Hosts should be sure to hang up the welcome banners in the classroom.

A. First, find your exchange partner and introduce yourself in German. If you can't find your exchange partner, ask around.

▶ *You:* Entschuldigung, ich suche Karl. Wo ist er?
Student: Er ist dort drüben.
You: Bist du Karl?
Karl: Ja.

B. Now introduce yourself to at least three other students. Use your list of questions and the information on their name tags to start a conversation with each of them.

Hast du das gewusst?

As in the U.S., it's customary for people in German-speaking countries to shake hands when they meet for the first time. But handshakes aren't reserved for introductions: friends often shake hands when they meet or say good-bye. Close friends often greet each other with a kiss on the cheek as well.

4. Schritt Dein Album

Add your list of questions and your name tag to your portfolio to keep as souvenirs of the first meeting with your exchange partner.

Noch etwas dazu

In German, introduce your exchange partner to one of the people in your group with whom he or she has something in common. Use the information from the **Noch etwas dazu** activity in Section B on page 12. Give your friend's name and tell your exchange partner what he or she has in common with your friend.

▶ Karl, darf ich meine Partnerin Jennifer vorstellen? Jennifer ist 14 Jahre alt und fährt auch gern Schi.

E Einen Ausflug planen

Along with meeting new people, your exchange trip includes an excursion to a site of interest in the German-speaking city you've chosen.

Brauchbares

- Encyclopedias
- Guidebooks for German-speaking countries
- Travel brochures and magazines
- Blank 3" x 5" index cards
- Colored markers
- Portfolio
- The World Wide Web

1. Schritt

Das Thema

A. To help you decide what type of site you'd like to visit, choose two topics from the following list that interest you.

Architektur	Kunst	Natur	Sport
Geographie	Märkte	Politik	Technik
Geschichte	Musik	Ruinen	Theater

B. Present your selections to the class and find two or three people who share your interests.

▶ *Student 1:* Findest du Theater interessant?
Student 2: Ja, Theater finde ich interessant.
Student 3: Nein, Theater finde ich langweilig.

Verknüpfungen

- ✔ Geographie
- ✔ Geschichte
- ✔ Kunst
- ✔ Technik

2. Schritt Was sehen wir uns an?

A. Now work with your group of three or four to find a site that reflects one of the areas of interest you've chosen. Use some of the resources listed in the **Brauchbares** box on page 19. The site must be in or near the city where the exchange trip is taking place. Based on the information you find, make a list of three reasons in German why you'd like to visit the site.

▶ *Topic:* Musik

Site: die Staatsoper

Reasons:
1. Die Sänger und Sängerinnen sind berühmt.
   The singers are famous.
2. Das Gebäude ist schön.
   The building is beautiful.
3. Es gibt viele Restaurants und Museen in der Nähe.
   There are many restaurants and museums nearby.

Suchen wir im Web!

Look back at useful Web sites you located in Section A on page 8. Check for information about specific places, such as museums or monuments, that you would like to visit in your city. Once you're on the Web site, you can look for information about the places you're interested in, links to additional pages within the site, and links to other sites with information about places of interest.

What if you already know a place in your city that you would like to know more about? Enter its name, such as *Pergamon Museum,* in the search function of your navigation software. If you only have a particular theme in mind, for example, historical monuments in Berlin, you can search via the city and theme. *Tip:* If your keyword is a phrase, put it in quotation marks. Remember not to put two words together in quotation marks unless you want to find them together as a phrase on a Web page.

Keywords

name of museum
"[name of city] + [theme]"

B. With your small group, present your site to the class in English or German.

3. Schritt Ansichtskarten

While visiting your site, you'll want to buy and write some postcards to your friends back home.

A. Working with a partner from your group, design two postcards showing the site you visited. Decorate one side of an index card with an image of the site. On the other side in the upper left corner include the name and a brief description of the place in German (or in English).

B. On your postcard, write a brief message in German to send to another German class in the visiting students' school in the U.S. If you're a host student, be sure to introduce yourself.

C. Include your research and your postcard in your portfolio.

Liebe Freunde,

schöne Grüße aus Wien! Die Hofburg ist sehr groß und schön. Sonntags singen die Wiener Sängerknaben in der Hofburgkapelle. Wien ist toll! Ich bin sehr glücklich hier, aber ich vermisse euch!

Tschüs!

Julia

Liebe Freunde,

ich bin die Karin, eine Freundin von Julia. Ich wohne in Wien. Julia hat die Stadt sehr gern. Ich auch!

Herzliche Grüße

Karin

Nützliche Vokabeln

Schöne Grüße aus [*place*]!	*Greetings from ___!*
Ich vermisse euch.	*I miss you (plural).*
[place] ist toll.	*___ is great.*
Tschüs!	*So long! Bye!*
Herzliche Grüße	*Best wishes, regards*
Viele liebe Grüße	*Love*

F Auf Wiedersehen!

The day for the visitors to return to the U.S. has arrived. It's time to say good-bye.

Brauchbares

- Colored markers
- Construction paper
- Portfolio

1. Schritt — Wir nehmen Abschied

On the day of the visitors' departure, say good-bye to the new students you've met during the exchange. Use the phrases in the **Nützliche Vokabeln** box and others you've learned in class. Since this is an exchange trip, you'll see each other again soon!

Nützliche Vokabeln

Alles Gute!	*All the best!*
Gute Reise!	*Have a good trip!*
Schreib bald!	*Write soon!*
Bis bald!	*See you soon!*

2. Schritt — Schreib doch mal!

A. After the visitors have returned to the U.S., both groups of students sit down to write notes to their new friends. If you were a visitor, write a thank-you note to your host. If you were one of the hosts, write a note to your guest, giving the date and time of your arrival in the U.S. for the second part of the exchange trip. Use one of the examples on page 23 as a model. The letters to hosts who have chosen a new identity should have their real names on the back so your teacher can distribute the letters.

Verknüpfungen

☑ Kunst

Liebe Karin,

Grüß dich! Wie geht's dir? Vielen Dank für alles. Dein Haus ist sehr schön, und deine Eltern und deine Schwester sind sehr nett.

Viele liebe Grüße

Julia

Liebe Julia,

schöne Grüße aus Österreich! Wie geht's dir? Ich fliege am 12. Oktober nach Amerika. Wir kommen um 16.00 Uhr an. Bis bald!

Herzliche Grüße

deine

Karin

B. Give your letter to your teacher, who'll deliver it to your exchange partner. Read the letter you've received. If you need help understanding it, consult your teacher.

3. Schritt Dein Album

Add the letter you've received to your portfolio. Now you have a complete record of your exchange trip! Decorate the cover of your portfolio and give it a title, such as **Meine Reise nach** ___ (*My trip to* ___).

PROJECT

2

Feste feiern, wie sie fallen

Using your knowledge of holidays, celebrations, and the cultures of German-speaking countries, you will help make a calendar, working in groups. Your work will be combined with that of other groups to make a yearlong calendar. In the process, you will:

- Research the major legal holidays of one German-speaking country or region and compare them to the U.S. legal holidays
- Determine what special occasions are observed in your chosen German-speaking country or region, including when, why, and how they are celebrated
- Pay special attention to one holiday that is common to all German-speaking countries and regions
- Use the information you've gathered to put together a holiday calendar that you can use throughout the year
- Hold a holiday celebration

Viel Spaß dabei!

Verknüpfungen

In the process of making a holiday calendar, you'll sharpen your skills in many areas.

- [x] Geschichte
- [x] Geographie
- [ ] Gesundheit und Ernährung
- [x] Kunst
- [x] Lernmethoden
- [ ] Mathematik
- [ ] Medien
- [x] Musik
- [ ] Naturwissenschaft
- [x] Technik

Look for the **Verknüpfungen** boxes throughout this project.

Warm-up: Fest- und Feiertage in den USA

Like every country, the U.S. has its **Feiertage** (*legal holidays*) as well as **Festtage** (*other special celebrations*). At these times, people in the U.S. commemorate occasions and traditions important to the entire country or to a particular region. Government offices and many businesses may close, and there may be public or private celebrations. Let's take a look at U.S. holidays, which can give you clues to what's celebrated in German-speaking countries.

Brauchbares

- Calendar with U.S. holidays
- Folder to use for the calendar project

A. Your teacher will divide the class into groups. Each group will make a calendar for a German-speaking country. In your group, use a calendar to make a list of holidays in the U.S. and give their dates.

B. You may get some of these days off, but do you know what each one celebrates? In your group, discuss in English or German the reason for each holiday and decide which of the following categories each holiday belongs to. Some holidays may fit in more than one category.

- Political—related to government
- Military—related to a war, armed victory, or veterans
- Civil—related to an event or an idea that is neither political nor military
- Religious
- Historical
- Other categories

c. When you've finished, report your findings to the class and discuss your ideas together. Put your notes in your calendar folder.

Hast du das gewusst?

We follow the Gregorian calendar, which was first introduced in 1582 and is used in most places in the world for business purposes. It's named after Pope Gregory, who improved the calendar originally developed by Julius Caesar. The Gregorian calendar is based on a solar year, the time that it takes the Earth to follow its complete path around the sun. A solar year is 365 days, 5 hours, 48 minutes, and 46 seconds long. The Gregorian calendar adds an extra day every four years to make up for the difference between the solar year and the 365-day calendar; that year is called a "leap year" (**Schaltjahr**).

A Feiertage im deutschen Sprachraum

The German-speaking countries wouldn't celebrate Columbus Day, of course, but do they have legal holidays like Thanksgiving or Independence Day? You're going to find out!

Brauchbares

- Books and magazines about international holidays and German-speaking people and cultures
- Guidebooks for German-speaking countries and regions
- German-English dictionary
- Legal Holidays Worksheet 2.A.1
- Holiday Comparison Worksheet 2.A.2
- The World Wide Web
- Folder

1. Schritt — Wie heißen die Feiertage?

A. Work with your group to find the major legal holidays of a German-speaking country or region, using some of the resources listed in the **Brauchbares** box. List each day in German with its English translation on Legal Holidays Worksheet 2.A.1 under **Feiertag**. As you do your research, record in German or English when and why each holiday is celebrated under **Datum** and **Grund**. Be sure to keep a list of the resources for later use.

B. In your group, categorize the holidays, using the same groupings you did for U.S. holidays—**politisch, militärisch, Gedenktag, kirchlich, geschichtlich**. Add any other categories that would apply. While your discussion may be in English, use the German names for the holidays and the categories. Record your results under **Art des Feiertags** on Legal Holidays Worksheet 2.A.1.

Verknüpfungen

- ☑ Geschichte
- ☑ Technik

Suchen wir im Web!

Official agencies of German-speaking countries are a good source of information about holidays in those countries. At the Government, Reference, Travel, or Society and Culture sections of a Web guide, use the keywords to the right to help you in your search about your country.

Keywords

"Botschaft + [name of country]"
Konsulat
name of holiday
Feiertage / Festtage

C. Now present your findings to the class. While your discussion may be in English, use the German names for the holidays. Be sure to put your worksheets in your calendar folder.

2. Schritt Vergleichen wir die Feiertage!

A. In your group, compare in English how U.S. holidays and those in German-speaking countries or regions are alike. Be sure to use the German names for the holidays. Do Americans and German speakers celebrate the same kinds of events? In English, record at least two similarities on Holiday Comparison Worksheet 2.A.2.

B. Now search for differences. What category do most German-speaking holidays belong to? What about U.S. holidays? Do Americans and German speakers celebrate comparable holidays but at different times of the year? Discuss and record at least two differences in English on Holiday Comparison Worksheet 2.A.2.

C. In English, present the similarities and differences to the class.

Hast du das gewusst?

Germans know how to make the most of holidays. In some **Länder** (*states*), citizens may get as many as 16 legal holidays off compared to 9–11 in the U.S. Major religious holidays such as Easter (**Ostern**), Pentecost (**Pfingsten**), and Christmas (**Weihnachten**) are each celebrated for two days. Also, if a holiday falls on a Thursday or Tuesday, Monday or Friday becomes a holiday, too. Germans also receive much more paid vacation—six weeks is considered standard, in addition to paid holidays. As a result, many Germans vacation in all parts of the world on a regular basis.

B Schatzsuche

Although you may not get the day off from school, you know that many other special days are celebrated throughout the year in the U.S.—Valentine's Day and April Fool's Day, for example. There are also many local holidays, such as Patriots' Day in Massachusetts, or Mardi Gras in New Orleans. Every country has such special days. What can you find out about such holidays in the German-speaking countries?

Brauchbares

- Books, guidebooks, and magazines with information about international holidays and German-speaking people and cultures
- German-English dictionary
- Special Days Worksheet 2.B
- The World Wide Web
- Folder

1. Schritt Was wird gefeiert?

In your group, research four special days or occasions that are celebrated in your German-speaking country. Gather all the information you can on these events. If possible, find pictures of people celebrating these holidays and of things connected with these celebrations. Use the materials listed in the **Brauchbares** box for help. For each day or occasion, fill in the chart on Special Days Worksheet 2.B.

Nützliche Vokabeln

Das feiert man [im Herbst].	*That's celebrated [in the fall].*
Das Fest findet am [*date*] statt.	*The celebration takes place on [date].*

Verknüpfungen

- ✔ Geographie
- ✔ Geschichte
- ✔ Kunst
- ✔ Technik

Suchen wir im Web!

How to find holidays will depend greatly on what you've chosen. Most Web guides do not have a section called "holidays," so look under sections labeled Culture, Social, or Society for references. You may want to refer to the Web sites of consulates and embassies, if you've already found some interesting information there. If you search by holiday name, remember it's best to use German names. Otherwise you'll be referred to holidays all over the world. Don't forget to bookmark useful Web sites for future reference.

Keywords

Festtage / Feiertage
name of holiday
"wtg-online"

2. Schritt Ideenaustausch

Now with your group, get together with another group in the class and share information. Take turns asking and answering in German, if possible, the following questions about the special celebrations in your countries.

> Wie heißt der Festtag? Wann feiert man? Warum feiert man? Wie feierst du diesen Feiertag?

3. Schritt Entwerfen wir ein Plakat!

Using the information and visuals you gathered in the **1. Schritt**, create a poster in German to advertise one of the special **Festtage** of your country. Include the date, name, and any other relevant information and symbols. Make it attractive, and hang it on the wall of your classroom for everyone to see.

Hast du das gewusst?

Summer in the German-speaking countries brings their version of the county fair to many areas. Whether it's called a **Schützenfest**, **Kirmes**, **Dom-**, or **Jahrmarkt**, such local fairs give the whole community a chance to get together and celebrate outdoors. Special events such as sports contests or folk-dancing exhibitions are often included, as is live music for evening dancing. Every fair features endless amounts of food, from traditional fare to a wide assortment of foreign foods. Fairground rides, games of chance, and souvenir stands round out the summer fair experience.

C Ein gemeinsamer Feiertag

It just wouldn't be July 4 without . . . a picnic at the lake? fireworks? a parade? What would you say? Each U.S. holiday has its own festivities. How do German-speaking people celebrate their holidays? Pick a holiday common to all groups and describe it.

Brauchbares

- Legal Holidays Worksheet 2.A.1
- Special Days Worksheet 2.B
- Books on international holidays
- Books on German-speaking people and cultures
- Guidebooks for German-speaking countries and regions
- German-English dictionary
- Folder

1. Schritt Das feiern wir ja auch!

You know the names, dates, and reasons for your group's holidays. Now you'll discuss what holidays the German-speaking world has in common.

A. As a class, take turns asking each other in German about the holidays celebrated in different German-speaking countries and regions. Refer to Worksheets 2.A.1 and 2.B and follow the model below to find out what holidays are common to all the countries studied. Make a list together.

▶ Feiern die Österreicher auch Ostern?
Ja, die Österreicher feiern Ostern.

▶ Feiern die Schweizer den Tag der Deutschen Einheit?
Nein, sie feiern den Tag der Deutschen Einheit nicht.

Verknüpfungen

- ✔ Geschichte
- ✔ Kunst
- ✔ Musik
- ✔ Technik

B. Select one common holiday that all groups will investigate. First discuss the possible choices. While your discussion may be in English, use the German names for the holidays. Choose a secretary to list the suggested holidays in German on the board. At the end of the discussion, take a vote. Voters for each holiday raise their hands and count off aloud in German. The secretary records the votes and announces the class choice.

▶ *Secretary:* Wieviele stimmen für [den Tag der Arbeit]?
Voters: Eins, zwei, drei, vier ...
(Repeat for each common holiday.)
Secretary: [Silvester] ist unser Lieblingsfeiertag.

2. Schritt Lieder, Tänze und Feuerwerk!

A. Now find out how your group's country celebrates the holiday your class has chosen. In your group, use some of the resources listed in the **Brauchbares** box to answer the following questions in English. You'll use the answers to prepare a brief report to the class.

1. How is the holiday celebrated? Are there private events with friends and relatives at home? Are there any public events, such as parades, fireworks, and dances?
2. Are any special foods served? Describe them.
3. Are there any special costumes or colors that people wear? What do the clothes or colors represent?
4. What special music or songs are played? Why? Provide examples, if you can.
5. What special places, symbols, or flowers do people associate with this day? Why? Provide examples, if you can.

Noch etwas dazu

Write a brief paragraph in German explaining how your group's country or region celebrates the holiday that your class has chosen. The holiday vocabulary in the Almanac will help you.

B. With your group, prepare a short oral and visual presentation in English or German about how your country celebrates this holiday and present it to the class. If your presentation is in English and you have a paragraph in German, include it here (see the **Noch etwas dazu** activity on page 33). Include any pictures, drawings, and music you found.

C. After each group has given its presentation, have a class discussion about the similarities and differences in the celebrations.

Hast du das gewusst?

By now you may know that April Fool's Day is called **der Erste April** in Germany, Austria, and Switzerland. As in the U.S., it's a day when children and adults play pranks on each other and exclaim **"April, April!"** ("April fool!"), when their practical jokes succeed. This tradition dates back to the Julian calendar established by Julius Caesar in 46 B.C. April 1 was the first day of the year until the Gregorian calendar later changed New Year's to January 1. People continued to give each other gifts as a joke on April 1. This joke became the custom of playing tricks on April 1.

D So ein schöner Kalender!

Now that you have all the information you need, it's time to decide on the final details and assemble your calendar.

Brauchbares

- The materials in your calendar folder
- Tagboard or butcher paper, markers, rulers, etc.
- A 12-month calendar covering the current school year
- The World Wide Web

1. Schritt — Was für Symbole?

Using your worksheets and the materials and notes in your folder, consider what you now know about each of the holidays in your German-speaking country—its purpose, the way it's celebrated, and the common colors and symbols that people use for it. With your group, decide how you want to represent each holiday on the calendar. You might draw something or use pictures that you found in your research.

2. Schritt — Die Aufgaben verteilen

You need to make some basic decisions on the actual making of the calendar. How will you divide the tasks?

A. In class, decide how you want to divide the work. Do you want each group to work on one part of the year, creating the grids and representing the holidays for these months? Or do you want each group to have a particular task? Make these decisions with the help of your teacher.

Verknüpfungen

- ☑ Geschichte
- ☑ Kunst
- ☑ Technik

B. Next, decide with the class how you want to set up the calendar pages. Be creative. Use the questions below to guide you.

- Where will the name of the month be? across the top? down the side? along the bottom?
- Will all the grids be the same color? different colors?
- Where will the names of the countries be listed? on the cover page?
- What art do you want to include to represent each month?

Remember that **Montag** is generally the first day of the week on a German calendar!

Hast du das gewusst?

In Austria and the Catholic regions of Germany, people celebrate their name days. Many people are named after saints since, by law, a child's name must be picked from an approved list of names. Each day of the year marks the feast of a particular saint or an important event in the Catholic Church. Saints' days are printed on many German calendars, and regional newspapers may list the day's saint and give a brief history. To mark the occasion, children receive cards, candies, or small gifts. To wish someone a happy name day, say: **Herzlichen Glückwunsch zum Namenstag!**

Suchen wir im Web!

Can you find your name day? If you don't find your first name, try your middle name. Having a name day is like having two birthdays a year!

Keywords

"Catholic calendar"
"Catholic Online Saints"

3. Schritt Los, an die Arbeit!

A. In your group, divide up the tasks of making the calendar pages, and get to work! Make sure you have all the information you need from the other groups.

B. Assemble your work as a class, making sure everything is in place. After your calendar is created, if you wish, add the name days and birthdays of your group members to your calendar.

C. Display the calendar and admire your handiwork. You've made a resource that you can use all year!

Nützliche Vokabeln

Das Fest findet am ___ statt.	*The celebration takes place on ___.*
Ich mag/Wir mögen ___ lieber.	*I/We prefer ___.*
Ich mag/Wir mögen ___ am liebsten.	*I/We like ___ the best.*
Mein/Unser Lieblingsfeiertag ist ___.	*My/Our favorite holiday is ___.*

4. Schritt

Unser Lieblingsfeiertag

Think about all the different **Festtage** and **Feiertage** that your class has discussed and decide which one is your favorite. In your group, take turns asking and answering questions, following the model below. When everyone has finished, determine the favorite **Festtag** or **Feiertag** of your group. Then take a class vote to determine the class favorite. If that celebration appears on your group's calendar, mark it in a special way.

▶ **—[Jan], welchen Fest- oder Feiertag magst du am liebsten?**
—Ich mag [Chanukkah] am liebsten. Und du?
—Ich? Ich mag [Ostern] am liebsten.

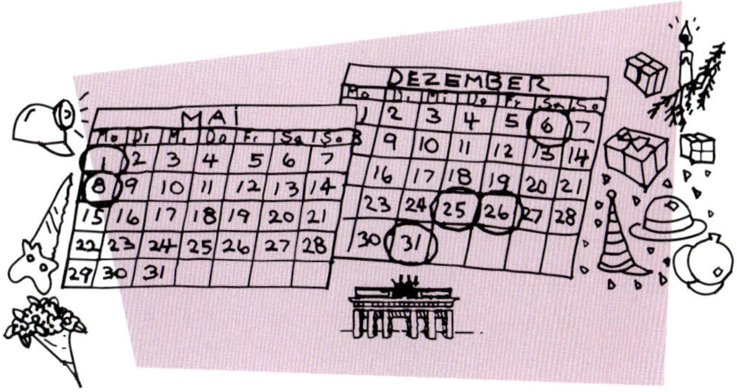

E Jetzt feiern wir!

After all the hard work you've done, you deserve to celebrate! Celebrate holidays the way German-speaking people do. Think colors, sounds, and excitement everywhere.

1. Schritt Welche Tage wollen wir feiern?

As a class, decide how you want to celebrate and organize the party. Do you want to celebrate the class's favorite holiday (see Section D, **4. Schritt**)? Do you want to celebrate the holiday coming up next on the calendar? Or do you want to celebrate a mix of the holidays you studied? Discuss the options with your teacher.

2. Schritt Die Organisation

You should now decide on the logistics of this celebration. What do you want to prepare for the celebration? Will you have guests coming to the party? How will you invite them? Where will you hold the party? Will there be food? How will you divide the work? Make sure you use your worksheets and the materials in your folders to help you present the holidays. You might want to choose a volunteer or two to prepare a checklist of what's needed and to supervise the preparation.

3. Schritt Amüsiert euch gut!

Has everything been taken care of? You are now ready to celebrate and answer questions about the holidays in German-speaking countries. Enjoy!

Hast du das gewusst?

Having been both a staunchly Catholic nation and the site of Martin Luther's Protestant Reformation, Germany has regions that have remained predominantly Catholic (**katholisch**) and others that are predominantly Lutheran (**evangelisch**). In Catholic regions, the pre-Lenten festival known as **Karneval, Fasching**, or **Fastnacht** includes private parties, public "roasts," parades, and lavish costume balls that continue until midnight on **Karnevalsdienstag**, the day before Ash Wednesday (**Aschermittwoch**). Traditionally Lutheran regions, on the other hand, celebrate holidays such as Reformation Day (**Reformationstag**) or Repentance Day (**Buß- und Bettag**).

PROJECT

3

Das ideale Schlafzimmer

In this project, you and your group will design your dream bedroom! At the end of the project, your class will award prizes to the best rooms in several categories. As part of this project, you will:

- Choose categories and make prizes for the room competition
- Design the style, color, and décor of your room
- Select appropriate furniture
- Prepare an exhibit and make a presentation of your room
- Hold a design festival and award the prizes

Bitte nicht stören!

Verknüpfungen

As you design your room, you'll sharpen your skills in many areas.

- [ ] Geographie
- [x] Geschichte
- [ ] Gesundheit und Ernährung
- [x] Kunst
- [x] Lernmethoden
- [ ] Mathematik
- [ ] Medien
- [ ] Musik
- [ ] Naturwissenschaft
- [x] Technik

Look for the **Verknüpfungen** boxes throughout this project.

Warm-up: Das gefällt mir!

A. Work with the same group of three or four of your classmates for this entire project. Each group member should bring in at least two photos or drawings of student rooms or bedrooms from magazines, catalogs, books, and so on. In German, describe each of your rooms to your group. Then as a group, write a list of the positive and negative features of the rooms.

▶ *Positiv*	*Negativ*
Das Bett ist groß.	Die Farben sind zu dunkel.
Der Teppich ist bunt.	Die Lampe ist alt.

B. Now, interview some other members of your class in German and find out which features appeal to them and which don't.

▶ Die Lampe ist alt. Ich finde sie nicht schön. Und du?
Ja, sie gefällt mir auch nicht.
Nein, ich finde sie toll.

C. In your group, share the information that you've gathered and add it to your list of positive and negative features.

▶ *Positiv*	*Negativ*
Der Teppich ist bunt. (Matt)	Die Lampe ist alt. (Alice)

D. Review your list of positive and negative features. Are there any features that were liked or disliked by more than one student? Circle them on your list and keep the list for reference when designing your room.

Hast du das gewusst?

People in the German-speaking countries like to adorn their houses or apartments with flowers. Buying flowers is as commonplace an activity as buying groceries. Generally customers purchase flowers in fresh-cut bouquets rather than in arrangements.

In addition to displaying flowers inside their homes, city dwellers grow them in window boxes or on their balconies or patios. In Austria, Switzerland, and Germany, people who live in large cities often own or rent a small plot of land on the outskirts of the city on which they grow flowers and vegetables. These small gardens, called **Schrebergärten,** provide a place for families to go and relax on the weekend and to get away from the hustle and bustle of the city. Some gardens even include a small structure that can house gardening tools and patio furniture or provide simple shelter.

A Der Wettbewerb

At the design festival, prizes will be given for the best rooms in several categories. Create these categories now so that you'll have a goal in mind as you complete the design of your ideal room.

Brauchbares

- Ballot Worksheet 3.A
- Cardboard or sturdy paper
- Scissors, tape, glue
- Computer and word-processing program
- Folder for storing worksheets and creative ideas

1. Schritt Die Kategorien

A. Working in your small group, brainstorm in German three possible prize categories to be used in your room competition. Be creative!

▶ lustig
bunt
originell
sehr modern

B. For each category, write a short description in English of the criteria that will be used when choosing a winner in that category.

▶ **bunt:** This room must contain at least three prominent colors in its décor and be bright and cheerful.

Verknüpfungen

☑ Kunst
☑ Lernmethoden

2. Schritt Stimmen wir ab!

Share your ideas for categories with your class. Vote as a class and choose four to eight categories to be used in the competition. Copy the categories the class chooses onto Ballot Worksheet 3.A. You'll use this ballot when it's time to vote.

3. Schritt Was gibt es zu gewinnen?

A. Divide the chosen categories with their descriptions among the groups in your class. Each group will make prizes to award to the winner of its categories. You may choose to make ribbons, medals, certificates, or trophies. Use the resources in the **Brauchbares** box to help you.

B. Put the prizes, the descriptions of the categories, and Ballot Worksheet 3.A away until the day of the competition. File the categories and descriptions in your folder.

Hast du das gewusst?

Bedding (**das Bettzeug**) in Austria, Switzerland, and Germany varies from the sheets and blankets used in the U.S. A bottom sheet is used to cover the mattress. On top of the sheet is a down comforter (**das Federbett**). The down comforter is covered with a sheet casing that buttons at the bottom and is removable for cleaning. The comforter and pillows (**die Kopfkissen**) are often aired on a daily basis by opening the bedroom window and hanging them on the window ledge.

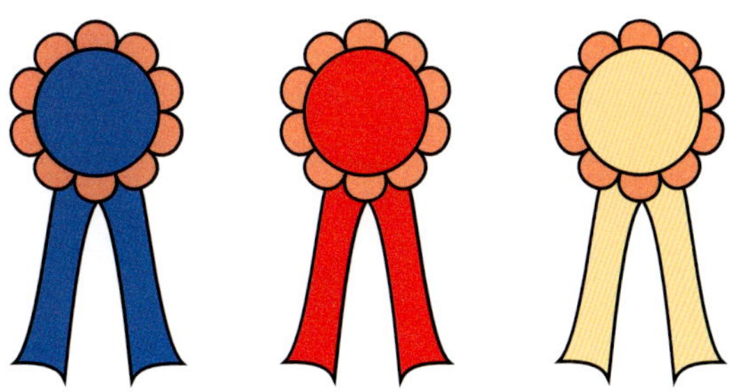

B Entscheidungen treffen

Now it's time to begin designing your ideal bedroom. You'll need to make some general decisions first. This is your chance to be creative!

Brauchbares

- Cardboard or sturdy paper
- Style Worksheet 3.B
- Magazines showing decorating ideas
- Art books or pictures of artwork from the German-speaking world
- Encyclopedias

1. Schritt Der Stil

Working with your group, you'll need to decide on the décor of your room. Do you want it to be traditional? futuristic? Should it have a theme, such as a particular movie, time period, or sport?

A. When you've chosen a style, write a description of it in English on Style Worksheet 3.B.

B. Now, consider how you will achieve this look. Will it be with wallpaper? a mural? furniture? On Style Worksheet 3.B, write a general description of ways that your style can be established in your room. When you're finished, put Style Worksheet 3.B in your folder. You'll make final decisions later. Make sure you choose specific competition categories.

Verknüpfungen

- ☑ Geschichte
- ☑ Kunst

Noch etwas dazu

Choose an influence from a German-speaking country to include in your room's décor, such as a **Bauhaus** or **Biedermeier** design, or a country style that might be found in a farmhouse in the **Schwarzwald** or a mountain chalet in the Swiss Alps. Record your ideas on Style Worksheet 3.B with the description of your room. Use the resources in the **Brauchbares** box to help you.

2. Schritt Die Farben

Now decide which colors will work best with this style. Maybe metallic colors would look great in your space-age room. Or perhaps you'd like bright blues to complement a nautical theme. Refer to the Almanac for a list of colors. Choose colors for the walls (**die Wände**), floor (**der Fußboden**) or floor covering, and even ceiling (**die Decke**). Record your choices in German on Style Worksheet 3.B.

3. Schritt Noch ein paar Details

Finally, decide what kinds of floor, window, and wall coverings you'll use in your room. Use the words for furniture and furnishings in the Almanac to help you. Record your choices in German on Style Worksheet 3.B, and place it in your folder.

C Die Möbel

Your ideal room wouldn't be complete without plenty of interesting furniture. Keeping in mind the style of your room, design your furnishings!

Brauchbares

- Decorating magazines, mail-order catalogs
- Catalogs from furniture and department stores
- Original drawings/descriptions of creative décor
- The World Wide Web

1. Schritt Wunschliste?

In your group, make general decisions about the furniture you'll want to have in your room. Make a list in German of the items and the quantities. Refer to the list of furniture and furnishings in the Almanac as needed.

▶ 1 Bett
2 Stühle
1 Schreibtisch

2. Schritt Beispiele finden

As homework or in class, look through decorating magazines, store and mail-order catalogs, and the Web to find some of the pieces of furniture on your list. Draw, print out, or cut out several options for each item on your list, so that your group has possibilities to choose from.

Verknüpfungen

- ☑ Kunst
- ☑ Technik

Suchen wir im Web!

Many furniture stores and companies advertise on the Web. Their ads often include pictures of their products. To locate such Web sites, try using a search engine with versions for German-speaking countries. For example, on Yahoo!, click on Germany at the bottom of the page. Follow the path **Handel und Wirtschaft**, **Firmen**, and **Haus & Garten**. You will find a list with many promising categories like **Möbel**, **Teppiche**, **Innenarchitektur**, and so on. Scan the descriptions of the Web sites and investigate those that look promising.

3. Schritt

Die idealen Möbel auswählen

Finally, in your group, choose the furniture items that you feel best complement your room's style. Refer to your list of furniture to make sure that you choose enough items. Save your pictures and drawings of furniture to prepare your room for the competition.

Hast du das gewusst?

Built-in closets are not as common in homes in the German-speaking countries as they are in the U.S. Most homes or apartments don't have a closet in the entryway. Typically, coats are hung on hooks on the wall. Bedrooms in Germany, Austria, and Switzerland don't usually have built-in closets either. Instead, clothes are hung in a tall wooden wardrobe (**der Kleiderschrank**) that often contains shelves on the inside and drawers at the bottom. If there is not enough space to hang pants or blouses, these items are neatly folded and placed on the shelves or in the drawers. Most bedrooms also have a chest of drawers (**die Kommode**) for storing clothing. **Kommoden** and **Kleiderschränke** come in all sizes and styles—from baroque to country to modern.

D So sieht mein Zimmer aus

Now decide how you're going to present your room visually during the design festival. Do you want to make a drawing of your room design and label the features in German? Or draw it using a computer drawing program? Do you think a poster with cut-out pictures will work best? Would you like to make a three-dimensional model of the room, such as a diorama? The possibilities are numerous!

Brauchbares

- Cardboard boxes
- Scissors, tape, glue, markers, paints
- Computer with drawing software
- Pictures or drawings of furniture

1. Schritt Wie wollen wir unser Zimmer darstellen?

Discover your group's talents and decide how to present your room to your class during the competition. If you're artistically inclined, consider using those talents to make a painting, drawing, or model of your room. If you enjoy working with computers, try out a drawing or paint program. Find a style of presentation that uses everyone's talents.

2. Schritt An die Arbeit!

Once your group has decided on how to present your room, it's time to get to work! Remember to include in some way all of the decisions that you made earlier on colors, style, and furnishings. Put them all together into a finished visual product, ready for the design festival.

Verknüpfungen

- ☑ Kunst
- ☑ Lernmethoden
- ☑ Technik

3. Schritt Beschreiben wir das Zimmer!

Finally, create short descriptive labels in German for your display. Label the furniture and furnishings, give your room a title, and highlight four or five features that make your room special. Prepare what each group member will say in German for your presentation.

Noch etwas dazu

Write a composition or poem in German describing the unique features of your ideal room. You may mount it, and then illustrate it.

E Der Wettbewerb beginnt!

The day of the design festival has arrived! Your room and those of your competitors will be on display. Today you will be both competitor and judge of the competition!

Brauchbares

- Prizes and descriptions of categories
- Ballot Worksheet 3.A
- Your room presentation

1. Schritt Die Kategorien überprüfen

Before starting the competition, review the categories that you recorded on Ballot Worksheet 3.A. by which the rooms will be judged. Each group will briefly read to the class the names and descriptions of its competition categories.

2. Schritt Das Zimmer ausstellen

Now it's time for the competition to begin! Display your room presentation and have each member of your group describe a few important features of your room to the class. After each group has given its presentation, take turns answering questions about your display and visiting the other displays. Be prepared to ask questions and make comments in German while you visit. Take notes on Ballot Worksheet 3.A as you view each presentation.

Verknüpfungen

☑ Kunst

3. Schritt Stimmen wir ab!

It's time to vote for the winner in each category. Each class member votes on each category and gives the completed Ballot Worksheet 3.A to your teacher, who will tally the results.

4. Schritt Die Preise verteilen

After the vote, the teacher awards a prize to the winning presentation for each category. Celebrate your victories! Display your group's presentation in the classroom.

Nützliche Vokabeln

Herzlichen Glückwunsch!	*Congratulations!*
der Sieger/die Siegerin	*the winner*
Der Preis für [ein sehr kreatives Zimmer] geht an ___.	*The prize for [a very creative room] goes to ___.*

PROJECT 4

Wer spielt mit?

Using your knowledge of games in the German-speaking world, you and your group will make a board game. In the process, you will:

- Make up questions and answers in German about daily life
- Research one or more German-speaking countries and make up questions and answers in English
- Write directions for the game
- Design and make a game board
- Test the game board and rules
- Share your game with your classmates

Du bist dran!

Verknüpfungen

In the process of making a game, and depending on what topics you choose for your game, you'll sharpen your skills in many areas, including these:

✔ Geographie	☐ Mathematik
☐ Geschichte	☐ Medien
☐ Gesundheit und Ernährung	☐ Musik
✔ Kunst	☐ Naturwissenschaft
✔ Lernmethoden	✔ Technik

Look for the **Verknüpfungen** boxes throughout this project.

Warm-up: Unsere Lieblingsspiele

You probably have a few favorite games. Why are they your favorites? Some people like short and simple games, while others prefer games that involve more complex strategy. Still others like the excitement of games in which luck is an important ingredient. Perhaps you prefer the physical dexterity and quick thinking that are part of video games. Find out what games you and your fellow group members like to play and why.

A. Form a small group of four to six students. Name your favorite games in English and explain why you like them. Read the **Hast du das gewusst?** box to find out the German names of some popular games.

B. In your group, brainstorm any German words and expressions you know that have to do with games.

C. In your group, talk in German about the types of games you prefer to play: for example, board, card, or computer games. The **Nützliche Vokabeln** box and the illustrations that follow will help you.

Hast du das gewusst?

Many popular German board games are probably familiar to you: **Dame** (*checkers*), **Halma** (*Chinese checkers*), **Schach** (*chess*), and **Stäbchen/ Mikado** (*pick-up sticks*). Many have the same name as in English, such as **Domino**, **Monopoly**, **Scrabble**, **Backgammon**, and **Trivial Pursuit**. One of the most popular German board games is **Nur keine Aufregung!**, also known as **Mensch ärgere dich nicht!** The aim is to get your four playing pieces to the center of the board. Dice are thrown to move your pieces, but other pieces along the way can block you or send you back to the start, evoking both frustration and fun!

Nützliche Vokabeln

spielen	*to play (a game or sport)*
Was spielst du gern?	*What [games] do you like to play?*
Ich spiele Trivial Pursuit gern.	*I like to play Trivial Pursuit.*
Ich spiele lieber Schach.	*I prefer to play chess.*

Schach spielen

Dame spielen

Brettspiele

Computerspiele spielen

Kreutzworträtsel lösen

Karten spielen

A Die Spielfragen

You've been asking and answering questions in German ever since you started studying the language. You may not realize it, but you can make a board game using those questions and answers—and that's what you're going to do!

Brauchbares

- 3" x 5" cards in one color
- Question Worksheet 4.A
- Folder or binder to compile Worksheets and other materials

1. Schritt Wie viel wisst ihr?

A. What kinds of questions can you ask in your game? Start with everything you've learned to say in German so far. Build on simple questions by adding a phrase, such as **auf deiner rechten/linken Seite** (*on your right/left*) or ask about someone's family members.

▶ Wie heißt du?
Wie heißt dieses Mädchen?
Wie heißt das Mädchen auf deiner rechten Seite?
Wie heißt deine Schwester?

How many variations of these questions can you come up with? Brainstorm and record a list with your group.

B. In your group, read through the topics under **Thema** on Question Worksheet 4.A. Check off topics that you know how to ask questions about. If you can think of any other topics, write them under **Andere Themen**.

Verknüpfungen

☑ Lernmethoden

2. Schritt Fragen und Antworten

Form pairs within your group and divide the topics among the pairs. Work with your partner to write 5–10 questions and answers in German for each of your topics. Record them on Question Worksheet 4.A. Use the back of the worksheet if necessary. Some questions will have only one possible answer (**Welche Farbe hat Schnee?**), while others will have answers that vary (**Wo wohnst du?**).

▶ *Question*: Wo wohnst du?
Possible response: Ich wohne in der Bahnhofstraße [15].

Question: Wie alt ist dein Bruder?
Possible response: Er ist ___ Jahre alt.

Question: Wie viele Geschwister hast du?
Possible responses: Ich habe ___ Bruder/Brüder und ___ Schwester/Schwestern.
Ich habe keine Brüder/eine Schwester.

Question: Wie/was ist deine Telefonnummer?
Possible responses: Meine Telefonnummer ist ___.

Hast du das gewusst?

In the U.S., one phone number is used throughout the country for police, fire, and medical emergency services (911). In Germany, there are different numbers for each emergency service. 110 is the number for the police (**die Polizei**), and 112 is for the fire department (**die Feuerwehr**). The number for emergency medical assistance differs from town to town and can be found by consulting local telephone directories. All these emergency numbers are toll-free and are listed on pay phones.

3. Schritt Fragen und Antworten überprüfen

A. Trade questions with another pair in your group and check each other's German. If you disagree or are unsure about what's correct, see if you can come to an agreement as a group before consulting with your teacher. Work together to make the best possible questions and answers.

B. Get back together with your group and look at the questions and answers that each pair has written. If possible, come up with additional questions and answers. Delete any duplicate questions.

C. Finally, write all the questions and answers on 3" x 5" cards of the same color. Use a separate card for each question and answer. Write the question on one side and its answer on the other.

Question		Answer
Wie viel uhr ist es? Wie spät ist es?	↔	Es ist 11 uhr 40. Es ist 5 nach halb 2.
Was ist dein Lieblingssport?	↔	(das) Schifahren.
Wie/Was ist deine Telefonnummer?	↔	Meine Telefonnummer ist 725-5234.
Wie geht es dir?	↔	Es geht mir gut! Ich bin krank.

B Kulturelle Fragen

Keep your game interesting and exciting by preparing questions in English about one or more German-speaking countries.

Brauchbares

- World map and maps of German-speaking countries
- Books and magazines about the history of German-speaking countries
- Encyclopedias and almanacs
- Travel magazines and brochures about the German-speaking world
- 3" x 5" cards in a color different from those in Section A
- Folder
- The World Wide Web

1. Schritt

Land und Leute

A. In your group, discuss what subjects relating to the German-speaking world seem interesting to you. You may know very little about some of them, so you might want to do a little research before choosing your topics. Below and on the next page are a few sample topics:

- The geography, history, and/or famous people of a German-speaking country
- Daily life in a German-speaking country: family, food, school, and pastimes

Verknüpfungen

- ☑ Geographie
- ☑ Lernmethoden
- ☑ Technik

- Popular German-speaking musicians and actors; film or music festivals
- Sporting events such as World Cup soccer
- Vacation (**der Urlaub**) destinations in Germany, such as the beaches and islands of **die Ostsee** (*Baltic Sea*) and **die Nordsee** (*North Sea*)
- Famous cities of German-speaking countries

B. As a class, decide if all the groups will make games based on the same topics, different topics, or a mixture of the two. Then, in groups or as a class, select topics. Decide whether one topic or many would work best with your game and whether you want to have a special challenge section or some bonus questions. Remember that the cultural questions and answers you prepare on the German-speaking world will be in English.

2. Schritt Interessante Tatsachen und Informationen!

Form pairs within your group and divide the research according to your group's preferences. Using the sources listed in the **Brauchbares** box on page 61, make up a list of 5–10 possible questions for each topic. Include pictures of famous places and things if you wish. Be sure to keep notes about the sources you use. You may have to go back later to find more information.

Noch etwas dazu

Make your game more challenging by creating some additional questions in German. Base your questions on expressions you already know.

▶ *You already know*	*Variation*
Was ist ___?	Was ist die Hauptstadt von Österreich?
Wann findet ___ statt?	Wann findet Deutschlands Nationalfeiertag statt?
Wie heißt ___?	Wie heißt der Schweizer Bundespräsident?
Welche Farbe hat ___?	Welche Farbe hat die Fahne von Luxemburg?

3. Schritt Fragen auswählen

A. When you and your partner have finished your list, trade questions and answers with another pair. Check each other's lists to make the best possible questions and most accurate answers. In your small group, read all the questions and answers and delete any duplicates.

B. Write your cultural questions and answers in English on 3" x 5" cards. Be sure to use cards of a different color from those used in Section A. Write the question on one side of the card and the answer on the other. If you wrote any cultural questions in German (for the **Noch etwas dazu** activity), file that list in your folder for the moment.

Hast du das gewusst?

German speakers love to play cards (**Karten spielen**). One popular children's game, **Schwarzer Peter**, is similar to Old Maid. Players ask each other for cards. The goal is to get all the members in a family—children, parents, and grandparents—so you can lay down your cards. German decks of cards (**Spielkarten**) often only go from the number 7 up. However, they do contain **das Herz** (*heart*), **das Pik** (*spade*), **das Kreuz** (*club*), and **das Karo** (*diamond*). Many popular games in Germany are familiar to Americans, such as **das Rommé** (*rummy*), **das Bridge**, **das Canasta**, and **der Skat**.

C Die Spielregeln

Like all games, your board game needs a set of rules. Look at other games to help you decide what the objective, the rules, and the organization of your own game will be.

Brauchbares

- World map and maps of German-speaking countries
- Several board games and their directions, particularly games that use information or questions on cards
- Rules Worksheet 4.C (2 per group)
- 3" x 5" cards in a third color
- Guidebooks for the German-speaking countries
- Folder

1. Schritt Ein Brettspiel analysieren

In your group, choose a particular game and spread out the board and playing pieces. Next, analyze the directions of that game by answering the questions on Rules Worksheet 4.C. Then discuss as a class what the rules of a game include and the order in which they should be explained.

2. Schritt Die ersten Entscheidungen treffen

What will be the goal of your game? How will you use your question cards? Make some decisions about the basic procedures and moves of your game. As a group, answer the questions under Basic Decisions on a second copy of Rules Worksheet 4.C, but this time apply them to your game.

Verknüpfungen

☑ Lernmethoden

Noch etwas dazu

Decide what to do with the cultural questions in German that you created in the **Noch etwas dazu** activity in Section B. Will they become a separate set of questions or will you combine them with one of the other sets? Write each one on a 3" x 5" card, the question on one side and the answer on the other. If you are using them in a different way from the other sets of cards, use a third color of cards; otherwise write them on cards of the same color as the set to which they belong.

3. Schritt Die Spielregeln entwickeln

Work with your group to develop some rules for your game. Study the questions under Rules of the Game on Rules Worksheet 4.C to help you make decisions. Write answers applicable to your game on your second copy of the worksheet. You'll probably want to revise some of your rules later as you perfect your game.

4. Schritt Die Anleitung lesen

In your group, check your directions against what you wrote on Worksheet 4.C. For example, should you add anything to what the players need to play the game? Have you changed your ideas about how to use the question cards? Record any additions or changes. Then write a first draft of your rules. Remember to be very careful about details.

Hast du das gewusst?

German has many colorful expressions that can be used for playing games, such as **Du hast Schwein gehabt!** (*How lucky you were!*), **Hals- und Beinbruch!** (*Break a leg!*), and **Toi, toi, toi!** (*Knock on wood*). Frustrated players may say **Es ist doch alles für die Katz!** (*It's all useless!*), **So ein Käse!** (*What nonsense!*), and if they really don't care anymore, **Das ist mir Wurst!** A sore loser may be called: **So ein Brummbär!** If you're out of luck, try some German lucky charms such as a **Marienkäfer** (*ladybug*), **Hufeisen** (*horseshoe*), or simply **Drück die Daumen** (*cross your fingers*). **Viel Glück!**

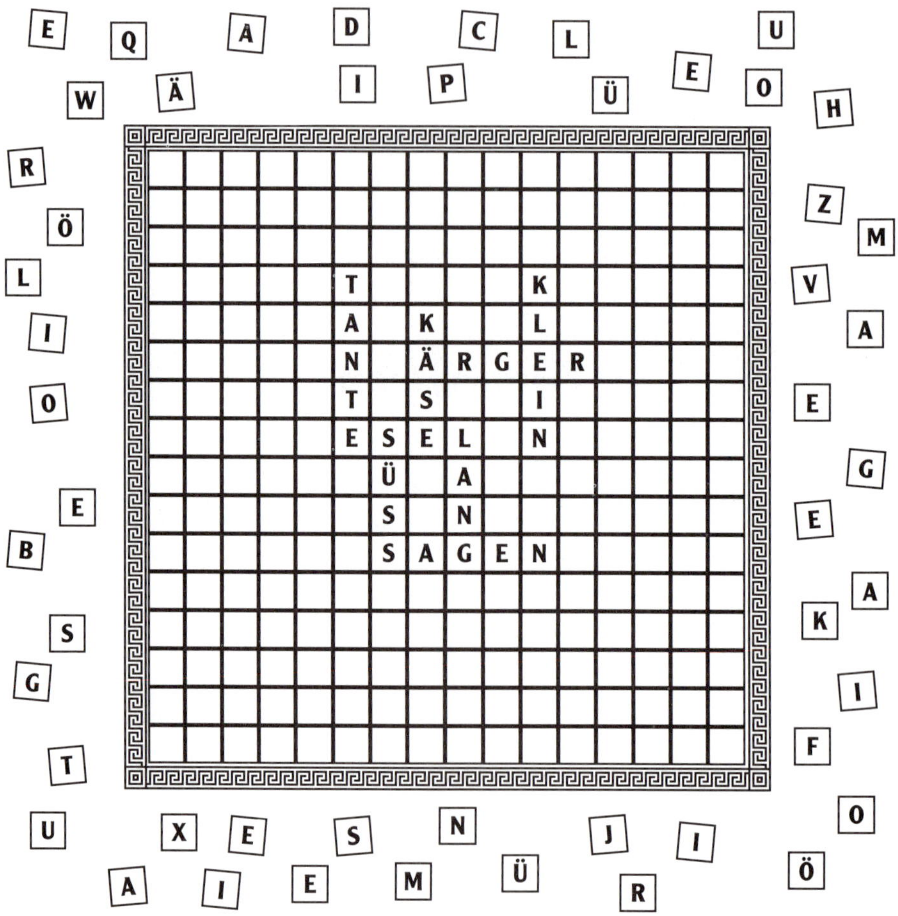

D Das Spielbrett

The game is starting to come together. Now that you have an idea of what the rules are going to be, you need to design the game board. It has to work with the rules you've written, or else you'll have to change some of the rules.

Brauchbares

- Several board games and their directions, particularly ones that use information or questions on cards as part of playing the game
- Analyzing a Game Board Worksheet 4.D.1
- First draft of rules for your game
- Our Game Board Worksheet 4.D.2
- Materials for creating the game board: colored markers, cardboard, file folders, poster board, tape
- Folder

1. Schritt Das Design analysieren

In Section C, you chose a board game and analyzed its directions. Now analyze the design of the same game's board. Spread out the board and playing pieces. Examine how the game board and the rules work together and identify features that had to be included on the game board because of its rules. For help, answer the questions under Features on Analyzing a Game Board Worksheet 4.D.1. Then complete the rest of the worksheet.

Verknüpfungen

- ☑ Kunst
- ☑ Lernmethoden

2. Schritt Notwendige Elemente

Since you've practiced looking for the features a game board might need, you're better prepared to design your own board. Keep Analyzing a Game Board Worksheet 4.D.1 nearby for reference. With your group, read through the basic game rules again. Look for features that *must* be included on your game board, such as directions that tell players:

- The starting place and the goal
- To go back or forward a number of spaces
- To take an extra turn or to skip a turn
- To choose a particular kind of card
- To go to a particular place on the board
- Where to put particular materials on the board

Record your decisions under Features on Our Game Board Worksheet 4.D.2.

3. Schritt Wie heißt das Spiel?

The name of a game often relates to its goal or to how it's played. In your group, brainstorm some ideas for a German name (you may have to do this in English). Record the suggestions, then take a vote. Record the group's choice under The Name of the Game on Worksheet 4.D.2.

4. Schritt Das Spielbrett dekorieren

A. Keeping in mind the features you *must* have on the game board, discuss with your group how you want the board to look. There are some examples of game boards on the opposite page. Maybe you can adapt one of them to fit your game or come up with something unique. Jot down your decisions under Design on Our Game Board Worksheet 4.D.2 and draw a sketch on Worksheet 4.D.1 if you'd like. Decide where to position the name of the game on the board and record that information too.

B. Now brainstorm ideas about how to illustrate some of the topics covered in your board game. What other kinds of decorations do you want to include? Write your decisions under Decorations on Our Game Board Worksheet 4.D.2. As you decide how to illustrate the game board, think about where you might find pictures that you can photocopy, cut and paste, or draw.

5. Schritt Die erste Skizze

Make a first sketch of the game board in the same size as the final board. Be sure to draw in all the shapes and use the actual colors. If there are labels or directions on the board, write some samples to see if there is enough space. Check the sports and games vocabulary in the Almanac for the German expressions you need. As a group, decide who will actually do the sketch. Will one person or a pair of students take full responsibility, or will each group member prepare a different part? Then make the sketch.

E

Das Tüpfelchen auf dem i!

Before you can create the final rules and make your game board, you need to do a test run. How well will your rules and game board work together?

Brauchbares

- Materials for playing pieces: stones, beans, marbles, dice, wooden/plastic pieces in various shapes
- Art materials, such as colored markers and glue
- Materials for the game board itself: cardboard, file folders, poster board, tape
- Container for the game: box or large envelope with a clasp
- Folder

1. Schritt

Der erste Versuch!

Use your rough draft of the rules and a sketch of the game board to try out the game. Choose one group member to record any needed changes to the rules or the board while the others play the game in order to find out what works and what doesn't.

2. Schritt

Die Generalprobe

In your group, make any necessary changes to the directions or the game board, then play the game again. This time players speak German during the game. Many of the needed expressions are in the sports and games section of the Almanac. Your group may choose to have non-playing members help players use German expressions, so

Verknüpfungen

- ☑ Kunst
- ☑ Lernmethoden

that they can play the game at a reasonable speed. Once again, have one group member record any problems, including additional German expressions that players will need to play the game. You don't need to think of everything that players might say, just expressions that they will have to use often.

3. Schritt Probieren wir's aus!

If students who know nothing about your game can play it by reading the rules, it really works! Ask another group to play your game while a couple of students from your group look on. Your group members can help the other students play your game and record any problems. If there are difficulties, make the needed revisions.

4. Schritt Ein Behälter

Since you're making this game for yourselves and others to enjoy, it would be a good idea to keep it in some kind of sturdy container. You might consider using one file folder for the game board, another for the rules, and plastic bags, a large mailing envelope with a clasp, or a box as a container for the game pieces.

5. Schritt Jetzt geht's los!

You're finally ready to put the game together. In your group, divide up the final tasks. Write a final description of the rules (make sure these are easy to read). Do you need additional German expressions for playing the game? If so, make a list. Draw the final game board on the cardboard or poster board provided. Gather any materials necessary for playing the game. Prepare the containers that will hold the game and put in everything you've made and collected for the game. You've worked hard and your game is now ready to share with other groups. Take your show on the road!

PROJECT

5

Eine Olympiade organisieren!

Using your knowledge of sports and the German-speaking countries, you and your classmates will organize your own mini-Olympics for German-speaking countries. In the process, you will:

- Decide which games to hold (Summer or Winter Olympics)
- Create and compete in 2–6 competitive events
- Prepare the opening ceremonies
- Design costumes or symbol cards and medals, and hold an awards ceremony
- Locate anthems and folk songs of the participating countries
- Hold your Olympic Games

You and your classmates will be grouped in committees and will work on many tasks at the same time to prepare for your mini-Olympics.

Schneller, höher, weiter!

Verknüpfungen

In the process of preparing and holding your Olympic Games, you will sharpen your skills in many areas.

- [x] Geographie
- [x] Geschichte
- [ ] Gesundheit und Ernährung
- [x] Kunst
- [x] Lernmethoden
- [x] Mathematik
- [ ] Medien
- [x] Musik
- [ ] Naturwissenschaft
- [x] Technik

Look for the **Verknüpfungen** boxes throughout this project.

Warm-up: Was wisst ihr über die Olympischen Spiele?

Brauchbares

- Olympic Sports Worksheet 5.W
- German-English dictionary
- Books about the Olympic Games
- Portfolio (a three-ring binder with pockets, file jacket, file folder) for each student
- The World Wide Web

A. Working with a small group, brainstorm in German a list of sports and write them under Part 1 on Olympics Sports Worksheet 5.W. Write each sport under the season in which it is played. Some sports may be played in more than one season.

B. In your group, decide which of the sports on your list are Olympic sports. Put a question mark next to any sport that you are uncertain about. Then decide if each sport is part of the Summer Games (**die Sommerspiele**) or the Winter Games (**die Winterspiele**) and list it under the appropriate heading in Part 2 of the same worksheet.

Hast du das gewusst?

Athletes from Germany have performed exceptionally well at the Olympic Games. A recent example is the 1998 Winter Olympics in Nagano, Japan. Germany won more medals than any other country (29): 12 gold, 9 silver, and 8 bronze medals. These medal counts clearly reflect the results of the reunification of Germany in 1989. As a separate country between 1968 and 1989, East Germany boasted a total of 515 medals in contrast to West Germany's total of 238.

C. Now work with your group to expand your list of Olympic sports. Use some of the resources listed in the **Brauchbares** box to find out what sports are played at either the Summer or the Winter Games. (Your teacher will tell your group which games it should investigate.) List at least five sports in German on your Olympic Sports Worksheet 5.W.

D. Finally, exchange information with the rest of the class and add the new information to Olympic Sports Worksheet 5.W. Put your worksheet in your portfolio.

Suchen wir im Web!

You can search the World Wide Web for information about where the Olympics have been held and what the geography and climate of the areas are like. This search is best conducted using a Web guide or catalog that will offer the option of performing the search in German. Guides written specifically for German speakers also exist. On the Web guide, look for Weather, Travel, and City sections or guides. Many city guides contain geographical and weather-related information. Remember to bookmark or note the Web address of any sites you may want to refer to later.

A Sommer oder Winter?

Cities and regions around the world compete for the privilege of hosting the Olympic Games. In choosing a location for the games, one of the most basic considerations of the International Olympic Committee is the geography of a region. For example, are the mountains suitable for Winter Olympic skiing events and do they receive sufficient snowfall? Are there appropriate bodies of water for Summer Olympic rowing and yachting events? You'll begin to organize your Games by deciding which Games you'll hold—**die Sommerspiele** or **die Winterspiele**.

Brauchbares

- World atlas
- Guidebooks for German-speaking countries
- Books about the Olympic Games
- Which Games? Worksheet 5.A.1
- Committees Worksheet 5.A.2
- Portfolio

1. Schritt — Wetter und Landschaft

Working with your group, brainstorm in German the kinds of climate and geography you think are needed to hold the Olympic Games. Continue with the same games—**die Sommerspiele** or **die Winterspiele**—that your group discussed in the Warm-up. Each of you should record the group's answers in Part 1 on Which Games? Worksheet 5.A.1. Share your information with the class.

Verknüpfungen

☑ Geographie

2. Schritt Wo haben die Spiele schon stattgefunden?

A. With your group, find out which German-speaking cities have hosted the Olympics in the past, using the resources in the **Brauchbares** box. Record the places in Part 2 of Worksheet 5.A.1 under **Wo**. List the games held in each location (**die Sommerspiele** or **die Winterspiele**) and the year.

B. As a group, choose one of the locations you listed. Find it on a map and then investigate and record its climate and geography. In Part 3 on the same worksheet, make a list in German of the features that you think made it a good location for the Olympics.

Nützliche Vokabeln

bergig	*mountainous*
flach	*flat*

C. Report your group's findings to the class. Ask your teacher to list the results of these reports on the board: two combined lists of features—one for the Summer Games and one for the Winter Games.

3. Schritt Winter- oder Sommerspiele?

A. In your group, start your search for a German-speaking city or town (and surrounding area) in which to hold *your* Olympic Games and research the climate and geography of your site. Would it be more suitable for the Winter or Summer Games? Perhaps your site is good for both games, only one, or neither **(weder die einen noch die anderen)**. Investigate each location, and record your answers in Part 4. If you discover your first choice is not suitable for any Olympics, select other sites until you locate a good one. Report your findings to the class.

B. As a class, vote on which Olympic Games you will organize and hold and where they will occur. Remember your Olympics will take place during the current season and at your location, so make reasonable choices. Record the class's decision under **Unsere Wahl** on the same worksheet.

4. Schritt **Wer macht was?**

This is your chance to decide which part of organizing the Olympic Games you'd like to work on. Read through Committees Worksheet 5.A.2 for an overview of the project. Decide which committee you'd like to be part of and get together with the other interested students. You can be an athlete as well as work on one of the other committees, but you'll have to organize whatever else you do around the times when you're taking part in a game. Keep your worksheet(s) in your portfolio as you work through your part(s) of the games.

B Welche Wettkämpfe?

As part of Committee B, it's up to you to decide what sporting events will be included in your games. You're going to design your own unique set of competitive events in which you and your classmates can participate.

Brauchbares

- Competitive Events Worksheets 5.B.1 and 5.B.2
- Athlete Information Worksheet 5.E.1 (filled in)
- Symbol Information Worksheet 5.F (filled in)
- Poster board, strips of paper or cloth, glue or stapler, felt-tip marker
- Computer with word-processing software
- Portfolio

1. Schritt Welche Wettkämpfe sollen stattfinden?

A. Committee B needs to design the five or six games or contests that are appropriate for the Winter or Summer Games that your class is organizing. At least *one* of the contests must involve a result whose distance or height needs to be measured. At least *two* should require physical activity and *two* should not. Divide any additional games however you want.

Choose a partner and think about the kinds of games you like. You may use parts of different sports or board games that you know or invent totally new games. Perhaps you want a mixture of individual and team games, some with a lot of physical action and others with basically none. Some ideas follow:

- Can you set up your own **Tour de France** (or other kind of bike race) in the school parking lot or around the school track? How about a tricycle race?

Verknüpfungen

- ✔ Lernmethoden
- ✔ Mathematik
- ✔ Technik

- Did you enjoy those three-legged races from grade school?
- How about a waltz/foxtrot dance contest or a yodeling contest?
- Why not have an ice sculpture contest to see who can create the most culturally authentic replica of a Bavarian castle?

Remember to keep in mind the information under **Unsere Wahl** on Which Games? Worksheet 5.A.1 as you develop your games. The events will occur in the place and at the season described there. Use the prompts under Description of a Game on Competitive Events Worksheet 5.B.1 to guide your designs. With your partner, record your answers in English on a separate sheet of paper for each game you make.

B. Now form a whole group again and discuss the games each pair has invented. As you choose the games, keep in mind the requirements laid out in Activity A.

After you choose the games, calculate the total number of winners so that Committee D knows how many medals to make. Remember that each contest will have first-, second-, and third-place winners and each player on a winning team will receive a medal. Then divide up the work of gathering the necessary materials for playing the games and keeping score. (See **2. Schritt** for creating a measuring tape.)

C. Now members of Committee B may get together with the athletes (Committee E) and briefly describe the games. Be sure to state how many students are needed for each team in the team events. Next, write an explanation in English of how each one is played and scored.

To test whether the directions are clear, review them with the athletes. (Note: the word "athlete" refers to all competitors, whether they are participating in a game requiring physical activity or a board game.) You will know who the athletes in each game are because each one will give your committee a copy of Athlete Information Worksheet 5.E.1. Have the athletes practice each game and if the explanations are unclear, revise them. Write the final directions, a complete list of materials, and how the game is scored on Competitive Events Worksheet 5.B.2, which will be used at the games.

D. Give each game a name. At your Olympic Games, the names will be announced in German and, for any non-German speakers watching, in English. The name might indicate the action involved in the game (such as Snowman Building—**Einen Schneemann bauen,** Sandcastle Building—**Eine Sandburg bauen**) or the number of people and the equipment the game requires (Two-Person Board game—**Zwei-Mann Brettspiel**). Record two of the German and English names on Competitive Events Worksheet 5.B.2. Finally, decide on the order in which the events will occur and write the numbers after Competition Number on the same worksheet.

To help the athletes practice, give them directions for the games in which they will compete. If a committee member wrote the directions on a computer, make multiple copies for your committee and the athletes.

E. Since the athletes at your games will all be speaking German, review the sports and games vocabulary in the Almanac. Brainstorm and add any phrases you think they may need to use while playing the games.

F. Now that Committee B knows what your contests involve, talk with your teacher as a group about where to hold them. Can they be played in the classroom? Do they require gymnasium facilities or a track? When you know where each game will take place, add that information to Competitive Events Worksheet 5.B.2. Make and post signs to tell spectators when and where the various games are taking place.

2. Schritt Wie weit? Wie hoch?

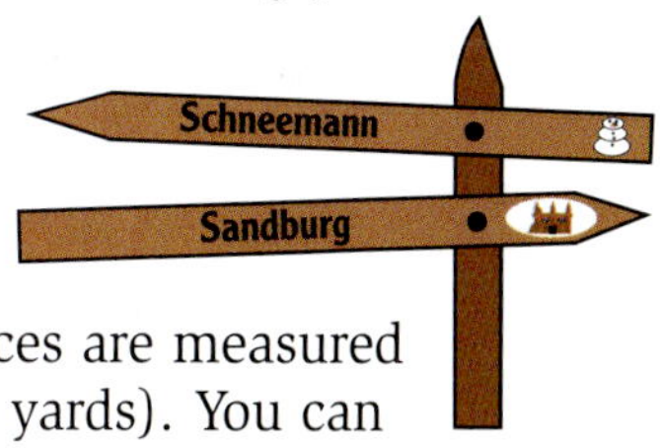

At international sporting competitions, distances are measured in meters rather than yards (1 meter = 1.094 yards). You can make your individual metric measuring tape by fastening together strips of paper or cloth and using a felt-tip pen to mark off 10-centimeter intervals (100 centimeters = 1 meter). A sample metric ruler is shown in the Almanac near the table of weights and measures. How many meters long does your tape need to be? Think about how far the athletes are likely to jump or how high they might build something.

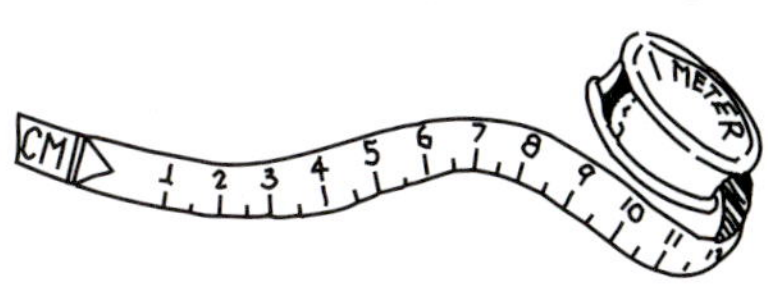

3. Schritt Die Rollen einteilen

As a committee, decide who will be the announcer and referee at the games. To allow as many students as possible on Committee B to participate at the games, change who plays these roles at each competitive event. Add this information to Competitive Events Worksheet 5.B.2.

- *Announcers:* The announcers tell the spectators in German a little about the athletes before each competition and announce the results. (Ask the athletes for their Athlete Information Worksheet 5.E.1. Ask the athletes' uniform designers for their Symbol Information Worksheet 5.F. You will use the information on these worksheets to introduce the athletes before they compete.) If the events at the actual games are held in different locations, be sure to include an announcement for the spectators about where the next competitive event will be held.
- *Referees:* The referees explain to the spectators in German how each game is played and scored. They supervise the game and take any necessary measurements. In addition, the referee keeps a record of each athlete's or team's score and gives that information to the announcer for Committee B. At the games, the referee will also tell the announcer for the Medal Committee the names of the first- (gold), second- (silver), and third-place (bronze) winners.

C Die Eröffnungsfeier mit allem drum und dran

The Olympic Games begin and end with ceremonies. These entertaining ceremonies include the parade of athletes, speeches, and performances that reflect the culture of the host country. Committee C is going to design the opening ceremony for your mini-Olympics.

Brauchbares

- Guidebooks for German-speaking countries
- Books on German-language legends, customs, and traditions
- Recordings of music from the German-speaking countries
- Competitive Events Worksheet 5.B.2 (filled in)
- Opening Ceremony Worksheets 5.C.1 and 5.C.2
- National Team Worksheet 5.E.2 (filled in)
- Portfolio

1. Schritt — Die Zeremonie beschreiben

As Committee C, discuss Olympic Game opening and closing ceremonies you have watched. Use the **Nützliche Vokabeln** box at the top of page 84 to help you speak German as much as possible. What happens at the ceremonies? What props are used?

Verknüpfungen

- ☑ Geschichte
- ☑ Kunst
- ☑ Musik

Nützliche Vokabeln

eine Fahne tragen	*to carry a flag*
ein Lied singen	*to sing a song*
eine Rede halten	*to give a speech*
die Sportler marschieren ein	*the athletes march in*
das Stadion	*stadium*
tanzen	*to dance*

2. Schritt Feste, Bräuche und Legenden

A. Individually, use some of the materials listed in the **Brauchbares** box to research celebrations, customs, or legends of the German-speaking host sites that can be performed or enacted at the opening of the Games. Record your findings in Part 1 of Worksheet 5.C.1.

B. Report your findings to Committee C, describing as much of the custom, celebration, or legend as you can in German.

3. Schritt Was könnt ihr am besten?

Make a list in German of all the talents you have in your committee. For example, who dances, sings, plays an instrument, draws, or speaks well in public? How can you combine the group's talents with a custom, celebration, or legend to make a special event that will be performed at the opening ceremony? Determine who will perform the special event. Record your decisions under The Performance at the Opening Ceremonies on Worksheet 5.C.1.

4. Schritt Wer, wie und wo?

As Committee C, decide how you want to organize the ceremony and where you will need to hold it. Will you require electrical outlets for plugging in a CD- or cassette player? If a dance is part of the performance, can the dance be done outside on the school grounds? How long will the ceremony be? When will the athletes parade in? In what order? When will the performance take place? Discuss your decisions with your teacher so that he or she can arrange an appropriate space for the ceremony.

Now use Opening Ceremony Worksheet 5.C.2 to list Committee C's tasks in German. Decide who will work on each one and record the names.

Record the order of the opening ceremony events in German on Opening Ceremony Worksheet 5.C.2. Then, in Part 3, list the order in which the national teams will march in the parade.

5. Schritt An die Arbeit

Now that your group has an idea of what the ceremonies will include and what your roles are, you need to work on the preparations, consulting with one another as you progress.

- *Speech writers*: Keep the opening speech brief and in German. Announce the various parts of the ceremony, such as the parade of the athletes and the performance. To announce the parade, you need the names of the countries represented at the games from Committee E. Also prepare a brief description of the performance. Find out from Committee B where the competitive events will be held, the name of each game, and the order in which the games will be played. Include this information at the appropriate time in the remarks.
- *Announcers:* Practice your speech and the announcements.

- *Performers*: What music, costumes, or props do you need? Plan and practice your performance.
- *Organizers*: Help everyone get organized in the parade.
- *Ushers*: Be prepared to direct spectators and athletes to their seats. Find out from the athletes what countries they represent and prepare a name sign for each country. On the day of the games, display signs that show where the athletes should sit. Prepare signs for spectator seating.

Once all preparations are made, hold a rehearsal to make sure everyone knows what he or she is supposed to do and when. For rehearsal purposes, members of your group should role-play the parts of the athletes and spectators.

Noch etwas dazu

Write a theme song in German for your games! Or choose a piece of classical, folk, or pop music, preferably from the host country. If necessary, the music could be from a different German-speaking country.

D Die Siegerehrung und die Medaillen

A moving moment of every Olympic event is when the officials place the gold, silver, and bronze medals around the necks of the winners. The design for Olympic medals is determined by the country hosting the games and may reflect the history, geography, or culture of that country. You're going to design the medals and the awards ceremony for your Olympic Games.

Brauchbares

- Books about the history of the German-speaking countries
- Books about the Olympic Games
- Colored markers, pencils, or paints; cardboard or poster board; scissors
- Competitive Events Worksheet 5.B.2 (filled in)
- Medals Worksheet 5.D.1
- Medals Ceremony Worksheet 5.D.2
- National Team Worksheet 5.E.2 (filled in)
- Computer with drawing software
- Portfolio

1. Schritt Wie sieht eine olympische Medaille aus?

Working with the other members of Committee D, locate at least one picture or description of an Olympic medal. Use some of the materials listed in the **Brauchbares** box. Note the games that the medal is from (the season, place, and year), its shape, and the words, images, and designs on it. Record the information in Part 1 of Medals Worksheet 5.D.1.

Verknüpfungen

- ✔ Geschichte
- ✔ Kunst
- ✔ Musik
- ✔ Technik

2. Schritt Originelle Medaillen entwerfen

A. Now it's time to individually design your own set of three medals. Decide on the shape and size. Measurements should be metric. You can use the metric ruler near the table of weights and measures in the Almanac. What words, images, or designs will be on each medal? Perhaps you want to include a well-known geographic feature or a historic place, event, or person on the medal. Will you hang the medals from chains, ribbons, or strings? Record your decisions for each medal in Part 2 of Medals Worksheet 5.D.1.

B. Present your design to your group, describing it in German. After all group members have presented their ideas, decide which design(s) will be used for your Games.

C. It's time to make the medals. Find out from Committee B how many winners you can expect. If any of the games are team events, find out how many people are on each team so you can prepare a medal for each team member. Record the information in Part 3 of Medals Worksheet 5.D.1.

3. Schritt Die Siegerehrung vorbereiten

As a committee, determine who will award the medals at the games. You may want a different presenter **(Moderator/Moderatorin)** for each game. The presenter(s) should be sure to get the winners' names and countries from the referees (see Committee B) at the games. Each presenter should prepare a short speech that he or she can use when awarding the medals and congratulating the winners. As a presenter, record your basic speech on Medals Ceremony Worksheet 5.D.2, leaving out the information about the athlete's (or team's) name and country until the actual games.

4. Schritt Der Probelauf

Once the medals and speeches are ready, rehearse the ceremony with members of your committee role-playing the winners. Check with students working on Committee F to be sure they have the national anthems ready. They will be responsible for playing them at the ceremonies. If possible, have them participate in your rehearsal.

Nützliche Vokabeln

die Medaillen	*the medals*
die olympische Medaille, -n	*Olympic medal(s)*
eine Medaille verleihen	*to award a medal*
Sie ist rund/oval.	*It is round/oval.*
Ihre Form ist rechteckig/ dreieckig.	*Its form is rectangular/ triangular.*
die Zeremonie	*the ceremony*
Sehr geehrte Damen und Herren	*Ladies and gentlemen*
Wir verleihen die goldene/ silberne/bronzene Medaille für ___ an [*name of student*].	*We award the gold/ silver/bronze medal for ___ to [name of student].*
Ich gratuliere herzlich./ Herzliche Glückwünsche!	*Congratulations!*

Hast du das gewusst?

The tiny country of Liechtenstein holds the world record of Olympic medals per capita. They proudly boast a total of 9 medals—not bad for a country of only 31,000 inhabitants! Alpine skier Hanni Wenzel was the first athlete from Liechtenstein to win an Olympic medal, a bronze medal for the slalom at the 1976 games in Innsbruck, Austria. In 1980, she went on to win three more medals—two gold medals for the slalom and the giant slalom, and one unexpected silver in the downhill. Her success was especially meaningful for both her family and Liechtenstein—fellow Olympic ski-team member and brother Andreas also won a medal in 1980—the silver for the men's giant slalom.

E Die Athleten

For athletes all over the world, competing in the Olympic Games is a great honor. On this committee, you are going to find out what the competitive events are, choose your contests, and practice for the games. You are also going to determine what German-speaking town and country you will represent and will make a flag (alone or with teammates) to carry in the opening ceremony.

Brauchbares

- World atlas
- Competitive Events Worksheets 5.B.1 and 5.B.2 (filled in)
- Opening Ceremony Worksheet 5.C.2 (filled in)
- Athlete Information Worksheet 5.E.1
- National Team Worksheet 5.E.2
- Paper, colored pencils, pens, or paints; ruler
- Guidebooks about German-speaking towns and countries
- A photo of yourself
- Portfolio
- The World Wide Web

1. Schritt Mannschaften bilden

A. Ask classmates on Committee B to present to your group the Olympic sporting events they've designed. Choose the event(s) in which you personally want to compete. Then in Committee E, arrange for the athletes who are taking part in team events to get together and form teams. Each team will represent a specific German-speaking country.

Verknüpfungen

- ✔ Geographie
- ✔ Kunst
- ✔ Technik

B. Committee B will ask you, as an individual and/or team member, to practice the games you are competing in to make sure the directions are clear. Once the committee has corrected any problems, you will get copies of the directions for the games. You can practice them on your own, with teammates, or with fellow competitor(s). Use the German vocabulary and phrases in the sports and games section of the Almanac as you do so.

2. Schritt — Woher kommst du?

A. As an individual athlete or as a team, decide which German-speaking country you represent. Next, group yourselves according to geographic areas. Using guidebooks and maps, individually select your hometown. Find out its population and one other interesting fact. If more than one athlete wants the same hometown, only one should include its population as part of the researched information. The other athlete(s) should look for two additional facts about it. Write your name and this information on your own Athlete Information Worksheet 5.E.1.

Next, meet as national teams and complete National Team Worksheet 5.E.2 in German. Also have athletes who are participating as individuals record information about themselves in Part 3. Committee F needs this information in order to make your uniforms. You'll need to get your uniforms from them for the opening ceremonies and the games.

Suchen wir im Web!

Using the Country guide or Travel section of a Web guide, look for the population and other interesting facts about "your" town or city on the Web. You might also want to use the Reference section of a Web guide and look for information in an encyclopedia. The keywords would be the name of the city or town.

B. During sporting events, information is often given about the contestants. Complete the rest of Athlete Information Worksheet 5.E.1 in German so that the announcers will have information to pass along to the spectators.

Noch etwas dazu

Write a short paragraph in German describing yourself for a press release. Include your age, where you're from, your hobbies, your favorite school subject, and your favorite food. Attach a photo to your description. With your group, display these paragraphs and photos in the classroom so that your fellow classmates can read up on the athletes who will be participating in the games.

Hast du das gewusst?

At the 1976 Winter Olympics in Innsbruck, Austria, skier Franz Klammer of Moorswald in Kärnten, Austria, beat Bernhard Russi of Switzerland by a mere 33/100 of a second in the downhill skiing event (**Abfahrt**) to win the gold medal. Interestingly, Klammer did not qualify for the Austrian downhill team for the Lake Placid Winter Olympic Games in 1980, but did make the team for the 1984 Winter Olympic Games in Sarajevo, Yugoslavia, where he finished 10th in the downhill. In the course of his career, Klammer won 26 World Cup skiing medals in addition to his Olympic Gold in 1976.

3. Schritt Die Fahnen

When Olympic athletes parade in the opening and closing ceremonies, one athlete from each country carries its flag. By obtaining a copy of Opening Ceremony Worksheet 5.C.2, you can learn where your country will march in the opening parade. Whether there is one person or several from the country that you're representing, find a picture of its flag. As a national team, decide who will make your flag and carry it in the opening ceremony. Then, using the picture you have found as a guide and some of the materials listed in the **Brauchbares** box, the selected athlete(s) will make the flag and attach it to a ruler. One very lucky athlete will carry it in the opening ceremony.

F

Der Einzug der Nationalmannschaften

In the opening and closing ceremonies, the Olympic athletes from a country wear similar clothing that often reflects their country or culture in some way. You're going to put together very simple costumes for the countries represented by the athletes at your games.

Brauchbares

- Books, magazines, and newspapers with information and pictures of the German-speaking countries
- Materials for making costumes or symbol cards
- Recordings of national anthems of the German-speaking countries and folk songs or popular music
- Competitive Events Worksheet 5.B.2 (filled in)
- National Team Worksheet 5.E.2 (filled in)
- Symbol Information Worksheet 5.F
- Portfolio
- Cassette player or CD player with speakers
- Computer with drawing software

1. Schritt

Was tragen die Athleten?

A. In your group as Committee F, get a copy of National Team Worksheet 5.E.2 from Committee E. Decide for which athlete(s) each of you will design a costume or symbol card. On your own, list each athlete's name, hometown, country, and the games in which he or she will take part on Symbol Information Worksheet 5.F.

Verknüpfungen

- ☑ Geschichte
- ☑ Kunst
- ☑ Lernmethoden
- ☑ Musik

B. Continue on your own. Use the materials listed in the **Brauchbares** box or textbooks to research costumes or symbols that you think may reflect the area(s) from which your athlete(s) come. For example, if your athlete(s) are from Lübeck, you may feel that **das Holstentor** is a typical symbol for the city. Record the information on Symbol Worksheet 5.F.

C. For each country that you chose, design a simple costume or hanging card that your athlete(s) can wear. It should reflect your research. At the games, be sure to give the card(s) to your athlete(s).

D. For each of your athletes, supply the information requested about your symbol in German on Symbol Information Worksheet 5.F. Use the **Nützliche Vokabeln** in Section D for help. Explain the meaning of the symbol in English and give the worksheet to the announcer on Committee B.

Noch etwas dazu

Explain the meaning of the symbol in German. Have the announcer at the games use the German instead of the English version.

2. Schritt Die Nationalhymne

When the medals are awarded at the Olympics, the national anthem of the gold medalist is played.

A. With your committee, locate a copy of the national anthem of each German-speaking country represented at your games. The German Department, the school library, or the town library may have the music you need. If you cannot find a particular piece, e-mail or write to the cultural attaché of the country's embassy nearest you. Explain in English why you need the music and express your thanks for any help the person is able to give you.

B. If you're not able to find a recording of a country's national anthem, locate and use a piece of music by a composer or musician born in the country.

C. Consult with Committee D about when you'll play the national anthems at the awards ceremonies.

G Die Spiele sind eröffnet

The big day is close at hand. To be sure everything is ready and that everyone knows how the games will proceed, you will have a dress rehearsal before holding the actual games.

Brauchbares

- All props, costumes, game equipment, music, and so on from Committees B–F
- Games Schedule Worksheet 5.G
- Computer with word-processing software
- Portfolio (three-ring binder with pockets, file jacket, or file folder)

1. Schritt — Ist alles fertig?

A. With your class, brainstorm a checklist in German of the preparations you have made for your Olympics. For example, the first items might be **die Spiele** and **Athleten informiert.** They indicate first that Committee B has designed the competitive events and has collected all the equipment. Committee B has also let the athletes know what the events are and what language they will need to use while participating.

B. Now each committee needs to check that it has obtained any information, props, and so forth needed from other committees.

2. Schritt — Das olympische Programm schreiben

As a class, prepare a list in German of what will happen and when it will happen at the games. To be sure that nothing is left out, use the list of preparations from **1. Schritt** and the phrases at the top of Games Schedule Worksheet 5.G for help. Record the final list on the same worksheet.

Verknüpfungen

- ✔ Geschichte
- ✔ Musik

3. Schritt Wir proben

Run through a rehearsal of the games, using your Games Schedule Worksheet 5.G as a guide. Because it is just a rehearsal, you may not wish to play each of the competitive events to completion. Rework or adjust any part of the games that isn't running smoothly.

4. Schritt Das olympische Feuer brennt

The big day is finally here. Hold the games. Good luck and have fun!

Noch etwas dazu

The Olympic Games have something for everyone—from the sportsmanship of those competing, to the artistic talent of those designing medals, to the organizational ability of those overseeing the games as a whole. Now write and produce a short newspaper about your Olympics.

In your group, write a short article in German about your part in the Olympics—for example, how the design of the athletes' clothing reflects their countries. If you have worked on more than one committee, choose your favorite to write about. Remember to give your article a headline. Ask your teacher to review your article. Then, as a class, assemble your newspaper. Your teacher will distribute it to the other German classes at your school.

PROJECT

6

Das ist unsere Schule

For this project, you and your group are going to create a school guidebook (**ein Schulhandbuch**), to be used by German-speaking exchange students. In the process, you will:

- Create a map of your school and label rooms, important features, and classroom items in German
- Prepare a profile of your school
- Present some of the extracurricular activities at your school
- Create a schedule of a typical day at your school
- Describe your school mascot (or create a new one) and invent a school cheer
- Design a school flag
- Videotape a guided tour of your school
- Create a title page and a table of contents for your school guidebook

Hereinspaziert!

Verknüpfungen

In the process of creating your school guidebook, you'll sharpen your skills in many areas.

- [x] Geographie
- [x] Geschichte
- [ ] Gesundheit und Ernährung
- [x] Kunst
- [x] Lernmethoden
- [x] Mathematik
- [x] Medien
- [x] Musik
- [ ] Naturwissenschaft
- [x] Technik

Look for the **Verknüpfungen** boxes throughout this project.

Warm-up: Schlagwörter

Before starting on your guidebook for German-speaking students, you'll need to do some brainstorming about your own school experience.

Brauchbares

- One three-ring binder per group with one pocket insert (or a 3-hole punched 9" x 13" manila envelope)

A. Form small groups. In your group, you can then each write three words in German that you associate with your school experience.

lernen *nett*
der Basketball

B. Exchange papers with a partner. Now write down one word that you associate with each word your partner wrote.

der Basketball—sportlich
lernen—viel
nett—Schulfreunde

C. Exchange papers with your partner again. Using the six words you now have on your paper, write one or two brief sentences about your school experience.

▶ Ich lerne viel in der Schule.
Unsere Basketballmannschaft ist sehr sportlich.
Meine Schulfreunde sind sehr nett.

D. Share your sentences with your small group.

E. As you complete each part of this project with your group, you'll be creating material for your group's school guidebook. Place your sentences in your group's binder.

A Eure Schule

For the first few days, it may be hard for new German-speaking students to find their way around your school. Drawing a map is the perfect way to help them out!

Brauchbares

- German-English dictionary
- Colored pencils or markers
- 3" x 5" (or 5" x 7") blank index cards

1. Schritt Der Lageplan

A. Working in a small group, draw a map of your school and the surrounding grounds. Your map needs to be large enough to accommodate small labels. If your school has more than one story, draw a floor plan for each story. If your own student handbook has a map, adapt it for this project.

B. Work together to see how many rooms, offices, and other features you can label in German on your map. Then use your German textbook or a German-English dictionary to label any remaining features. Identify at least five classrooms by the names of the subjects taught in them.

C. Get together with another group and compare your maps. Have you forgotten anything important?

Verknüpfungen

☑ Kunst
☑ Lernmethoden

Hast du das gewusst?

The German grading system is based on a 6-point scale. A grade of 1 is excellent (**sehr gut**), 2 is good (**gut**), 3 is satisfactory (**befriedigend**), 4 is passing (**ausreichend**), 5 is unsatisfactory (**mangelhaft**), and 6 is unacceptable (**ungenügend**). Both 5 and 6 are failing grades. Grades are based on class performance, written tests, and quizzes. There is a lot of pressure to receive good grades because university admission is very competitive.

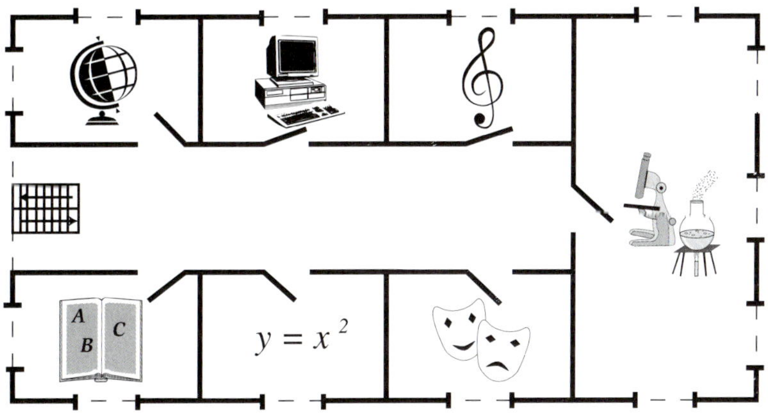

2. Schritt Weitere Wörter lernen

A. Create bilingual flashcards to help the new students learn the names of some rooms, offices, and other features of your school. In your group, make eight flashcards with the German name on one side and the English on the other.

B. With your group, create eight bilingual flashcards for items in your German classroom (desk, chair, bookcase, chalkboard, clock, and so forth).

3. Schritt Das Schulhandbuch vorbereiten

Put your group's school map into the guidebook binder. Place your group's flashcards in the pocket insert of the binder.

B Allgemeine Informationen

A map provides a general picture of what your school looks like. A school profile, or an outline of different characteristics, can help new students see at a glance what life is like at your school.

Brauchbares

- Statistical information about your school
- German-English dictionary
- School Profile Worksheet 6.B
- The World Wide Web

1. Schritt Zahlen und Fakten

Gather some basic statistics about your school.

A. Answer the questions in Part 1 of School Profile Worksheet 6.B. Ask your school librarian, teachers, or administrators to help you find this information.

B. In your group, compare your answers to Part 1 of Worksheet 6.B. If your answers differ, find out why. What sources did you each use? Then compare your answers with those of other groups.

Verknüpfungen

- ☑ Mathematik
- ☑ Technik

Suchen wir im Web!

If your school has its own Web site, look for the information there. Ask your teacher for the school's Web address if you don't know it.

2. Schritt Die Fächer

In addition to a general overview, the new students will appreciate a guide to the specific subjects offered at your school.

A. As homework, create a chart like the one below.

Fach	Ist es ein Pflichtfach?	Beschreibung
Englisch	*ja*	*macht Spaß*
Naturwissenschaft	*ja*	*interessant*
Kunst	*nein*	*einfach*

1. In the first column, list in German ten subjects at your school that you have taken or will take. Turn to the Almanac for a list of courses and subjects.
2. In the second column, indicate whether or not you're required to take the subject this year (**ja** or **nein**).
3. In the third column, write down one adjective or phrase in German that you think best describes each subject.

B. In German, compare your chart with those of others in your group. Are all of your required subjects the same? How similar or different are your descriptions of the subjects? Are the descriptions positive?

Nützliche Vokabeln

Welche Fächer hast du dieses Jahr?	*What classes are you taking this year?*
Hast du ___ ?	*Are you taking ___ ?*
Ich habe ___ .	*I'm taking ___ .*
Wie ist ___ ?	*What's ___ like?*
Hast du es als Pflichtfach?	*Is it a required class for you?*

C. In your group, divide the subjects you have listed in your charts into three categories: academic (**die akademischen Fächer**), arts (**die künstlerischen Fächer**), and other subjects (**die anderen Fächer**). Then list at least three subjects under each category in Part 2 of School Profile Worksheet 6.B. Include descriptions as well. One member of your group should record the group's answers.

D. Add your group's School Profile Worksheet 6.B to your school guidebook.

Hast du das gewusst?

The German and U.S. school systems offer similiar academic opportunities but are set up quite differently. At the age of 10, German students have four educational choices: to attend **Hauptschule**, **Realschule**, **Gymnasium,** or **Gesamtschule.** The latter most closely resembles a U.S. high school, with students of all academic inclinations. **Hauptschule** is for students who want to learn a trade, while **Realschule** prepares students for practical fields such as computer technology, accounting, or banking. Students who plan to study at a university attend **Gymnasium** and graduate with their **Abitur** (the equivalent of a 2-year college degree) at the age of 19. All students receive their **Schulabschluss** (*school diploma*) after the 10th grade.

C Die Freizeitaktivitäten

The German-speaking students may want to get involved in extracurricular activities. Introduce them to some of the organizations and teams at your school.

Brauchbares

- Extracurricular Activities Worksheet 6.C

1. Schritt Die Sportarten

A. In your group, write a list in German of at least six sports teams or intramural sports your school has. Organize your list according to season (fall, winter, spring, or summer) on Extracurricular Activities Worksheet 6.C. Refer to your textbook and the list of sports in the Almanac.

B. Now take your own survey of five classmates in other groups to find out what their favorite school sports are. Report your findings to your group. On Extracurricular Activities Worksheet 6.C, record which sport seems to be the most popular in your class. One member of your group should record the group's answers.

2. Schritt Die Arbeitsgemeinschaften

A. As a group, find out what school clubs and organizations each of your group members belongs to. List them in German on Extracurricular Activities Worksheet 6.C. Next to each club or organization, write a brief description of it in German. Refer to the list of clubs and organizations in the Almanac.

Verknüpfungen

☑ Lernmethoden

B. Now get together with another group and exchange information. Add any new information to Extracurricular Activities Worksheet 6.C.

Nützliche Vokabeln

die Arbeitsgemeinschaft (AG)	*club* (lit. *work group*)
In welcher AG bist du Mitglied?	*What club are you a member of?*
Ich bin Mitglied der ___-AG.	*I'm a member of the ___ club.*
Was machst du in der ___-AG?	*What do you do in the ___ club?*
Ich arbeite bei der Schulzeitung mit.	*I work on the school newspaper.*
helfen	*to help*
nachdenken über	*to think about*
organisieren	*to organize*
üben	*to practice*
vorbereiten	*to prepare*

C. Add Extracurricular Activities Worksheet 6.C to your group's guidebook.

Hast du das gewusst?

Extracurricular activities are not as common in the German school system as they are in North America. Music, foreign languages, and sports are among the most common and popular **Arbeitsgemeinschaften** for German high school students. Schools usually do not have a stadium or a swimming pool and will send students to use town facilities for activities such as swimming. Most students belong to sport clubs outside their schools. The local city or town usually runs these clubs. Generally each town or district has a few teams (soccer, basketball, gymnastics) that compete in regional or national competitions. When going to gym, students say: **Ich gehe Sport treiben**.

D Ein typischer Schultag

Help the German-speaking students experience a typical day of classes at your school. Assist them with schedules and directions.

Brauchbares

- School map (from Section A)

1. Schritt Dein Stundenplan

A. Create a chart with the days of the week in German across the top and the times corresponding to your class periods down the left side.

B. Create a model schedule for new students at your school by filling in the chart in German with your own school schedule. Add room numbers to indicate where each class meets.

Hast du das gewusst?

Students in small towns and rural areas that do not have their own schools usually travel to the closest school by public transportation. School buses provide transportation only to students from villages that do not have a train station. If students happen to live in a city, they take public transportation—buses or the subway—to school. Depending on how far they live from school, students can be seen walking, riding bicycles, or, if they are old enough, riding mopeds.

Verknüpfungen

- ✔ Geographie
- ✔ Lernmethoden

2. Schritt Enschuldige, wo ist ...?

A. Now help students find their way from one class to the next. Using your schedule and your group's school map, write directions in German so that the new students can find their way from:

- the main entrance to your first class
- your first class to your second class
- the cafeteria to your first class after lunch
- one class to any other class on your schedule

▶ Wie kommt man von der Cafeteria zum Fachraum Algebra, Zimmer 207?

Geh rechts um die Ecke.
Dann geh geradeaus bis zur Turnhalle.
An der Turnhalle, bieg links ab.
Geh die Treppe hinauf.
Algebra ist im dritten Klassenzimmer auf der linken Seite.

B. Work in pairs. Give one set of your directions to your partner, who will trace the route you describe on your school map. Reverse roles.

Nützliche Vokabeln

zu Fuß gehen	*to walk*
bis zu/zum/zur [+ *noun*]	*until, to the* [+ *noun*]
die Treppe hinauf-/hinuntergehen	*to go up/go down the stairs*
der Korridor	*hallway*
rechts/links	*to the right/left; on the right/left*
auf der rechten/linken Seite	*on the right/left side*
abbiegen	*to turn*
geradeaus	*straight ahead*
überqueren	*to cross*

C. Put your schedule and directions into your group's binder as samples for the visitors.

E Die Schule anfeuern

Students have many ways of expressing their school spirit. At a football game, for example, there may be a school mascot that represents the team. The cheerleaders try to inspire the crowd and support the athletes. Help the new German-speaking students catch your school spirit!

Brauchbares

- Colored markers
- German-English dictionary

Nützliche Vokabeln

die Mannschaft	*team*
der Fan	*fan*
das Team anfeuern	*to cheer for a team*
das Maskottchen	*mascot*
das Team unterstützen/anfeuern	*to support/cheer a team on*
Hurra für unsere Schule!	*Hooray for our school!*
Zicke, Zacke, Zicke, Zacke! Hoi! Hoi! Hoi!	(a German cheer)

Verknüpfungen

☑ Kunst
☑ Musik

1. Schritt Das Maskottchen

In your group, draw your school mascot and describe it in German. Use your current school mascot or create one of your own. Then present your mascot to the class.

▶ Unser Maskottchen ist ein Tiger. Er ist groß und furchterregend. Er ist gelb und schwarz gestreift.

Noch etwas dazu

How does your mascot represent your school? With your group, write a sentence in German that describes both your mascot and your school.

▶ Der Tiger und mein Gymnasium sind stark, groß, intelligent …

Hast du das gewusst?

Because team sports are not common at the high school level in German-speaking countries, students who are interested in sports generally follow the activities of local and regional sports teams. Two mascots that would be well known to young German soccer fans are the goat (**Ziegenbock**) that represents FC Köln and the red devil (**Roter Teufel**) that represents Kaiserslautern. The players from Kaiserslautern (**die roten Teufel**) wear red uniforms and are known for their "devilish" way of playing. Both teams are among Germany's best soccer teams.

2. Schritt Hurra!

A. In your group, decide whether you're going to write a cheer for your whole school or for one team or organization at your school. Then brainstorm action verbs in German related to your school, your team or organization, or your mascot. For example, if your mascot is a tiger, you might come up with verbs such as **laufen** or **springen**.

B. Now brainstorm some adjectives that describe your school, your team or organization, or your mascot. For example, **schnell**, **stark**, and **gefährlich** are adjectives that might describe a tiger. One member of your group should record the group's answers.

C. Finally, combine some of the verbs and adjectives you brainstormed into a simple, but energetic school cheer, such as the one shown. Have your teacher review your group's cheer. Then teach it to the rest of the class.

D. Add your school cheer and the picture and information about your mascot to your school guidebook.

F Die Schulfahne

Countries, states, schools, and organizations are often represented by a flag or banner. The colors and designs on these flags are usually carefully chosen to symbolize the ideals of the groups they represent.

Brauchbares

- An encyclopedia or almanac
- Colored markers
- Construction paper
- The World Wide Web

1. Schritt — Die Fahne der USA

As a class, discuss the significance of the symbols and colors of the U.S. flag.

1. Welche drei Farben hat die amerikanische Fahne?
2. Sind diese Farben wichtig? Was bedeuten sie?
3. Wie viele Sterne gibt es auf der Fahne? Warum?

Hast du das gewusst?

In the German-speaking countries, the national flag is never used as fabric for clothing. To do so would be considered highly disrespectful. In the same way, people don't hang flags inside or outside their homes, and schools usually don't display a flag either. Such actions would be considered too extreme. Flags appear on government buildings only on national holidays and for special events.

Verknüpfungen

- ✔ Kunst
- ✔ Geographie
- ✔ Geschichte
- ✔ Technik

2. Schritt Die Fahnen der deutschsprachigen Länder

Working with your group, look in an encyclopedia or your German textbook and select the flag of one German-speaking country. List in German the colors and symbols on the flag. What values or history do you think the colors and symbols might represent? Discuss your ideas in English. Consult an encyclopedia to find more information about the flag you chose. How does this information compare with your own ideas about the flag? Present your findings to the class in English.

Suchen wir im Web!

To find out more information about the flag you've chosen, search the World Wide Web using a Web Guide.

Keywords

"flags of the world"

3. Schritt Eure eigene Schulfahne entwerfen

A. Create a flag for your school or town. With your group, make a list in German of colors that you might want to include on your school flag. Next to each color, write what it could represent. You could include your school colors and perhaps add one or two more.

▶ Weiß = die Wahrheit
Gold = die Qualität

die Streifen (m.pl.)

B. Now draw some symbols that you think would represent your school. Next to each symbol, write in German what it stands for. You could include your school mascot or an important feature of your town or school. Use your imagination!

▶ der Löwe = die Kraft
die Sterne = die Ziele

C. Using your lists of colors and symbols, draw your flag or make it out of construction paper.

Noch etwas dazu

Write a brief explanation in German of the colors and symbols on your flag and how they represent your school or town.

▶ **Unsere Fahne ist zweifarbig. Weiß steht für Wahrheit. Gold steht für Qualität. In der mitte der Fahne gibt es einen Stern. Der Stern steht für unsere Ziele weil die Schüler hier viel erreichen wollen.**

4. Schritt Das Schulhandbuch vorbereiten

Explain your flag to the class. Display your flag in the classroom. Create a small version of your flag and add it to your group's school guidebook, along with your description of its colors and symbols.

G Eine Videoführung

Schools and towns attract students or residents by providing colorful informational brochures, videotapes, or even CD-ROMs about their schools and community facilities. Introduce the new German-speaking students to your school by videotaping your own guided tour.

Brauchbares

- School map from Section A
- German-English dictionary
- Video camera and blank videotape
- Construction paper, poster board, or colored paper
- Heavy-duty elastic band
- Computer with word-processing program

1. Schritt — Die Entscheidungen

A. With your group, review the map you made of your school and school grounds in Section A. Make a list of the rooms, offices, and features of the school that should be shown in your video tour.

B. Consulting your teacher, find two teachers willing to appear in your video. Teach them each a short greeting in German (for example, **Guten Tag** or **Willkommen im Mathekurs**).

Verknüpfungen

- ☑ Medien
- ☑ Technik

2. Schritt Die Kommentare

Working with your group, write one or two sentences in German to introduce and describe each of the teachers, rooms, and features you've chosen to highlight in your video. For each one, consider what significance it has for your school. Are there any relevant facts or statistics you can share? For example, how long has the biology teacher been at your school? When was the computer lab opened?

▶ Frau ___ unterrichtet seit zehn Jahren im Gymnasium.
Das Computerlabor ist neu.
Unsere Turnmannschaft ist die beste im Bundesland.

Noch etwas dazu

Find someone in your school (other than your German teacher!) who speaks German. Videotape a brief interview in German with her or him. You might ask for some advice for the new students.

3. Schritt Wichtige Details

A. With your group, plot the route you will take in taping your video tour. Use the descriptions you wrote in the **2. Schritt** to put together a short script for your video. Have the students in your group introduce themselves at the beginning of the tour.

B. Decide together how you will divide up the roles of director, narrator, and camera operator. You may want to share a role or change with each new scene.

C. Create the title and credits of your video tour using construction paper or poster board, or use attractive fonts from a word-processing program and print them out on colored paper.

4. Schritt Achtung, Aufnahme!

Finally, you're ready to tape the video tour of your school. It should be about three to five minutes long. All of the narration should be done in German. Remember to speak clearly! Rehearse your tour at least once before you begin taping. When your video tour is complete, show it to your class; then include it in your completed school guidebook, along with your script. Use a heavy-duty elastic band to "attach" your video to your guidebook.

H Die letzten Kleinigkeiten

To complete your school guidebook, make it easy to use by adding a title page, a table of contents, and page numbers.

Brauchbares

- School guidebook binder
- Construction paper and colored markers
- Computer with word-processing program

1. Schritt Die Titelseite

In your group, create a title page for your school guidebook using colored markers and construction paper or a computer word-processing program. Include the following useful information:

- Name, address, and phone number of your school
- Your group members' names and the date
- Other names, phone numbers, and office numbers that new students may need (the school nurse, principal, guidance counselor, and so on)

Hast du das gewusst?

School schedules for a typical classroom day vary from region to region within Germany. The school day runs generally from 8:00 A.M. to 1:00 P.M. However, students may stay longer if they are involved in an **Arbeitsgemeinschaft.** In addition, students stay in the same classroom all day except for lab classes, art, and gym. Teachers travel from room to room. Classes are generally 45 minutes long with a 5-minute break between classes.

Verknüpfungen

✔ Kunst
✔ Technik

2. Schritt

Das Inhaltsverzeichnis

Make a table of contents. Assign each item in your guidebook a page number so that new students will be able to locate the information quickly and easily. On a separate sheet of paper, list each item in your school guidebook and add page numbers.

3. Schritt

Es ist soweit!

Insert your title page and contents page into the front of your school guidebook binder. Congratulations on a job well done!

PROJECT

7

Das ist jetzt Mode!

Using your knowledge of clothing and German-speaking culture, you and your group will produce a fashion show. In the process, you will:

- Find examples of what German-speaking teenagers are wearing and compare their clothing styles with those of American teenagers
- Set up your own fashion design house
- Take on different roles for the preparation of the show
- Make a program and advertisement for the show
- Add decoration and music to the show
- Hold the fashion show

Jetzt wird Maß genommen!

Verknüpfungen

As you create your fashion show, you will sharpen your skills in many areas.

- [ ] Geographie
- [ ] Geschichte
- [ ] Gesundheit und Ernährung
- [x] Kunst
- [x] Lernmethoden
- [ ] Mathematik
- [x] Medien
- [x] Musik
- [ ] Naturwissenschaft
- [x] Technik

Look for the **Verknüpfungen** boxes throughout this project.

Warm-up: Latzhose oder Minirock?

Do you want to use your imagination and have some fun? You are going to be a fashion designer and present your unique creations at a show. Your clothing and accessories can show your interests, the kind of person you are, or just be for fun. Let's get started by talking about what you like to wear and where you like to shop.

Nützliche Vokabeln

Hast du ___ gern? Magst du ___?	*Do you like ___?*
Gefällt dir ___?/Gefallen dir ___?	*Do you like ___?*
Mir auch./Mir auch nicht.	*Me too./Me neither.*
tragen	*to wear*
die Boutique, -n	*small shop, boutique*
das Einkaufszentrum, -zentren	*mall, shopping center*
die Herren-/Damenbekleidung	*men's/women's clothing*
im Internet einkaufen	*to shop on the Internet*
der/die Jugendliche, -n; der Teenager, -s	*young person; teenager*
das Kaufhaus, ¨-er	*department store*
die Klamotten (*pl.*)	*clothes (slang)*
die Kleidung (*no pl.*)	*clothing*
die Ladenkette, -n	*chain store*
die Marke, -n	*brand, name*
das Modegeschäft, -e	*women's clothing store*
die Modezeitschrift, -en	*fashion magazine*
das Schaufenster	*store window*
einen Schaufensterbummel machen	*to go window shopping*
der Second-Hand-Laden, ¨-	*second-hand clothing store*
das Sonderangebot, -e	*sale, special offer, bargain*
im Sonderangebot	*on sale*
der Versandhauskatalog, -e	*mail-order catalog*

A. Do you prefer comfortable clothes? Do you like the latest fashions? In a small group, discuss in German the kinds of clothes and accessories you prefer to wear. Here are a few sentences to get you started.

▶ Was für Kleidung trägst du gern / am liebsten?
Am liebsten trage ich bequeme Kleidung.
Ich trage nicht gern Kleider. (Ich mag nicht Kleider tragen.)
Ich interessiere mich sehr für Mode!

Hast du das gewusst?

In 1853, German-born Levi Strauss moved to San Francisco to make his fortune in the dry goods business. One of his customers was a tailor named Jacob Davis. Davis decided to strengthen all the stress points in his pants with rivets, and the idea was an immediate hit. Although Davis wanted to take out a patent on his invention, he didn't have the $68 he needed to file the papers. So he enlisted Levi Strauss as his business partner, and the rest is history.

B. Where do you usually shop for clothes? in department stores? discount stores? clothing stores? through catalogs? In a small group, talk in German about your shopping habits.

▶ Wo kaufst du deine Kleidung?
Ich kaufe meine Kleidung am liebsten bei ___ . Und du?

C. Do you look at clothing ads? Where are you likely to look for the kind of clothes you like? In a newspaper, a special magazine, or elsewhere? In your small group, continue talking in German about your shopping habits.

▶ Ich lese Modezeitschriften wie [*name of magazine*].
Ich schaue mir die Werbe-Spots auf *MTV* an.
Ich gehe ins Internet und gucke mir dort die neue Mode an.

A Jugendliche und Mode

Traditionally styles came from Europe and then became popular in the U.S. Like many other businesses, however, fashion is now more international. Since World War II, the U.S. has become more and more influential in fashion. You know what U.S. teenagers wear, but what about German-speaking teenagers? Investigate the fashions in the German-speaking world.

Brauchbares

- Clothing Comparison Worksheet 7.A
- German-language magazines (Some, such as *Oskar's,* are published in both German and English.)
- Catalogs from German mail-order businesses, such as *Quelle* und *Otto*
- German-English dictionary
- The World Wide Web
- A folder to compile your worksheets and materials for this project

1. Schritt Was trägt man jetzt so?

Individually or in pairs, use some of the items listed in the **Brauchbares** box to determine what German-speaking teenagers are wearing. Then complete the information in Part 1 of Clothing Comparison Worksheet 7.A.

Verknüpfungen

☑ Medien
☑ Technik

Suchen wir im Web!

Check if the search engine or Web guide you're using has a German version. If so, try using both German and English. A German search engine finds many documents that are available in both German and English. For this search, a Web guide is particularly useful. In your searches, remember to use German words, especially with German search engines. It's also possible to find stores and boutiques by searching a particular region of the country. Some fashion magazines have Web sites, too. Remember to bookmark or record the addresses of the sites you like, so you can find them again later.

Keywords

Versandhaus
Mode
Modezeitschriften
Touristik / Fremdenverkehr

Hast du das gewusst?

Department stores such as Kaufhof, Karstadt, and Hertie have existed in most German cities for decades and offer stylish, affordable clothing. Outlet stores, the latest trend, are also sprouting up. But since quality rather than price dictates German shopping habits, many people still prefer to shop in small, independent shops that specialize in better quality clothing. Unfortunately, due to competition from designers' own boutiques, big chain stores, and mail-order businesses, such shops have trouble staying in business.

2. Schritt Vergleichen wir einmal!

In your group, discuss in German what you have discovered, answering the questions in Part 2 on Clothing Comparison Worksheet 7.A. How are the clothes of German-speaking and American teenagers alike or different? What are the most popular colors and types of clothing? Refer to the Almanac for clothing and colors.

▶ Jugendliche in den USA und in Deutschland tragen gern T-Shirts.

In der Schweiz ist die Farbe lila sehr „in".

Im Gegensatz dazu ist die Farbe schwarz sehr gefragt in den USA.

B Vorbereitungen für die Schau

Before your fashions hit the runway, there are many decisions to make and many things to prepare. First, you'll need to decide the kind of clothing your group wants to create and present in the show. What about clothes of the future, or regional costumes, or simply casual clothes? You'll also have to decide how you want to present them.

Brauchbares

- German-English dictionary
- Picture dictionary in German or multiple languages
- Fashion Show Decision Worksheet 7.B
- The World Wide Web
- Worksheet folder

1. Schritt Ein Modehaus mit eigenem Stil!

A. Fashion reflects a variety of styles and functions. In your group, think about and discuss in German the overall idea of your fashion collection. Use the questions and suggestions under **Die Ideen** on Fashion Show Decision Worksheet 7.B to come up with an outline of your collection. Be sure to record your decisions by checking the boxes or writing some additional ideas.

B. Fashion designers have to have a house name! What's yours going to be? Something unusual like **Cyber-Moden** or something very impressive like **Modehaus Kurfürstendamm?** Write the name of your design house on Fashion Show Decision Worksheet 7.B.

Verknüpfungen

☑ Lernmethoden

Cyber-Moden

Modehaus Kurfürstendamm

Aschenputtels Boutique

2. Schritt Wie organisieren wir die Modenschau?

Keeping in mind the decisions your design house made in the **1. Schritt**, discuss as a class—in German—how to organize the show. Use the questions and suggestions under **Die Organisation der Modenschau** on Fashion Show Decision Worksheet 7.B for help, and record your choices.

3. Schritt Wie nennen wir die Modenschau?

Next you need to choose a name for your fashion show. As a class, brainstorm names for the show. Vote for your favorite name and write your class's decision on Fashion Show Decision Worksheet 7.B. Put your worksheets in your folder.

Hast du das gewusst?

Düsseldorf is the traditional center of German fashion design, although trend-setting designers can also be found in Hamburg, Berlin, and Vienna. Karl Lagerfeld, one of the most famous German designers, has designed for Chanel, Chloé, and Fendi and started his own label in 1984. Hamburg's Jil Sander is famous for elegant contemporary city clothes. Clothes from other German fashion houses such as Escada, Joop!, Hugo Boss, and Austria's Helmut Lang are also in demand worldwide.

C An die Arbeit!

Being a fashion designer means you have a chance to do different things. Everyone will help design and assemble the fashions. Modeling, writing fashion descriptions, and so on, however, will be divided among group members to be sure that everything gets done. Keep the different choices in mind as you select what you want to do. You can't model and comment at the same time.

Brauchbares

- Materials such as cardboard, construction paper, feathers, cloth, rope, ribbon, plastic, glue, markers, tape, staplers, scissors
- German-language newspapers, magazines, mail-order catalogs
- German-English and picture dictionaries
- Fashion Show Decision Worksheet 7.C
- Worksheet folder

1. Schritt — Die Designer und ihre Kreationen

Now comes the fun part, making those fashions! Everyone in your fashion design house will work together to create them.

A. Keep your fashion theme in mind as your fashion house brainstorms ideas for actual fashions in English. List the items you decide to create on Fashion Show Decision Worksheet 7.C. Then allow models to select what they will model. Write their names on Worksheet 7.C. You need to know who will wear each item, so that you can make the clothes "fit." Finally, decide on the order in which your house will show its fashions and record the information on the worksheet.

Verknüpfungen

☑ Kunst

B. You may use all kinds of materials to make your fashions—paper, foil, or leather, for example. You may make an entire piece of clothing or add to an existing one. In your group, make a list of who will bring in which materials to make your fashions. There are more suggestions in the **Brauchbares** box.

C. It's now time to actually create your collection. Don't forget to let the models try the outfits on before the show so you can make any necessary adjustments.

2. Schritt Die Models

At the same time you're creating your fashions, you need to decide who will be modeling them.

A. Step right up! Who's ready to play the role of a model, or a **Model,** as they also say in German? How can you resist the opportunity to wear some of these gorgeous new styles? On Fashion Show Decision Worksheet 7.C, write the model's name next to the item he or she will present.

B. Each model may wear one or more of the fashions during the show.

3. Schritt Die Ansage

When designers bring their fashions to the runway, they do more than show their designs—they describe and comment on them as well. A vivid description of each model's outfit will help capture your audience's attention.

A. In your fashion house group, divide the creations among pairs of students. On Worksheet 7.C, record who will comment on what item. In pairs and using the materials listed in the **Brauchbares** box, research how fashions are described. As you read, jot down expressions that you might want to use to talk about your own creations. Refer to the illustrations on the next page for ideas.

B. Then, work with your partner to answer these questions about each item you'll be describing.

1. Um welches Kleidungsstück geht es hier?
2. Wie heißt das Model, das es vorführt?
3. Welche Farbe hat das Kleidungsstück?
4. Aus welchem Material ist es?
5. Zu welchen Gelegenheiten trägt man es?

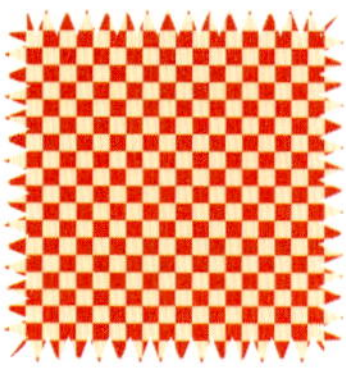

kariert

geblümt

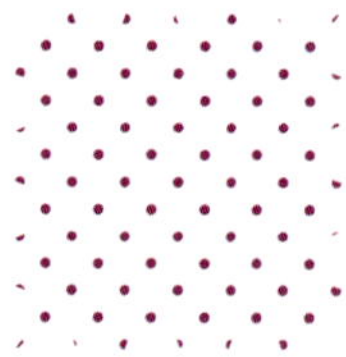

getupft

gestreift

bedruckt

C. In pairs, write an introduction for each of your fashion(s), using the information above. The example below shows one way the information collected might introduce a model and the fashion he or she is wearing.

▶ … Und hier ist unser Super-Model Jeremy.
Jeremy sieht aktuell, modisch und attraktiv aus.
Er trägt ein T-Shirt, einfach schwarz, mit einem Aufdruck von seiner Lieblingsgruppe ___.

Noch etwas dazu

Expand the description by adding more detail. The answers to these questions may help.

1. Zu welcher Tageszeit trägt man dieses Stück?
2. In welcher Jahreszeit trägt man dieses Stück?
3. Warum steht das Kleidungsstück diesem Model so gut?

D. Practice reading or saying your part in the fashion show aloud.

D Das Programmheft und die Werbung

Organizers of various kinds of shows often advertise their productions. A program will then help the audience follow what's happening. One half of the class will work on the Program Committee, the other half on the Publicity Committee.

Brauchbares

- Worksheets 7.B and 7.C
- Program and Publicity Worksheet 7.D
- Plain 8½" x 11" paper, poster board, and markers
- Newspapers and magazines that include clothing for teenagers
- Catalogs from German mail-order businesses
- German-English and picture dictionaries
- Worksheet folder

1. Schritt Wen laden wir ein?

As a class, discuss in German whom you want to invite to your fashion show. Do you want to present your creations to other German classes, families, teachers, and so on?

2. Schritt Was steht auf dem Programm?

Verknüpfungen

- ✔ Kunst
- ✔ Medien
- ✔ Technik

A. In your Program Committee, brainstorm a list of all the information that should be included in the program. Check with your teacher about your options for the place, date, and time of the fashion show before listing this information. Remember that German speakers often state time according to a 24-hour clock for events such as this.

B. Now complete the information in Part 1 of Program and Publicity Worksheet 7.D. The information on Fashion Show Decision Worksheets 7.B and 7.C will also help you. As you make decisions about the program, remember to:

- Plan what the cover will look like
- Determine who is responsible for keyboarding and duplicating the program
- Coordinate your information with the Publicity Committee

Nützliche Vokabeln

stattfinden	*to take place*
aufregend	*exciting*
faszinierend	*fascinating*
das Ereignis, -se	*event*
die Vorstellung, -en; das Spektakel, -	*show*
auf dem Laufsteg laufen	*to walk down the runway*

3. Schritt Die Werbekampagne

An important fashion show needs a good advertising campaign. It's time to get the word out! Decide how you want to advertise the fashion show—with flyers, through posters, or by some other means. If you want to use your school public address system or your school Intranet, read the suggestions in B and C on the next page.

A. In your Publicity Committee, using materials listed in the **Brauchbares** box on page 133, look for ads for various kinds of events—plays, concerts, and so forth. List the kinds of information these ads contain. Then discuss in German the information needed to advertise your show. Complete the information on Part 2 of Program and Publicity Worksheet 7.D. Jot down any English or German expressions that might help you write an ad. Make sure you coordinate your information with the Program Committee.

B. How about making a radio ad? If you have German-language radio stations in your area, listen to some of their ads. Otherwise, try ads on English-language radio stations. Decide how you're going to present the information in your ad—through the voice of one announcer? in the form of a conversation? Write, practice, and record your ad. Don't forget to use background sound effects!

C. If your school has an Intranet, use it as a quick way to get the word out about your fashion show. Since not everyone can read German, be sure to post your ad in English, too. Using the information you've gathered, write the details in both languages. Use descriptive words and/or art to make the ad more interesting. Before you send off the final copy, be sure to proofread it. Everyone in the whole school will read it!

Hast du das gewusst?

Many people in the German-speaking world still like to wear traditional outfits for special occasions. A women's outfit often consists of a traditional dress or **dirndl** with a long skirt, apron, and form-fitting laced bodice, a white blouse, and perhaps a short jacket of boiled wool. A man's outfit (**der Trachtenanzug**) tends to be dark green, brown, or black, and can include a long jacket or vest of wool or leather, a loose traditional shirt of linen or cotton with embroidery, and pants or the famous **Lederhosen** with suspenders, sometimes topped off with a traditional Tyrolean hat (**der Tirolerhut**).

E Die letzten Vorbereitungen

You're about to invest time and effort into the finishing touches that can make the difference between a good show and a great one—the music, the decorations, and a dress rehearsal to make sure everyone knows what to do.

Brauchbares

- Poster board or plain butcher paper
- Art supplies such as markers and construction paper
- Musical instruments, music tapes, or CDs
- German-English dictionary
- Video camera or tape recorder and blank tapes

1. Schritt Der Zeremonienmeister

Next up is finding a master of ceremonies to open and close the show and to introduce each fashion design house. Select one of your classmates for this role. Then, as a class, brainstorm what should be included in his or her speeches. The master of ceremonies will then finalize the text on his or her own.

2. Schritt Die Musik

Verknüpfungen

- ☑ Kunst
- ☑ Medien
- ☑ Musik

Now form a Music Committee to select and list the music that you are going to play. Choose a committee member to tell the Program Committee what the music program will be. Arrange when and where you are going to rehearse. Be prepared to play the music during the dress rehearsal of the show.

3. Schritt Die Ausstattung

You will also need to form a Decorating Committee. Use your imagination and have fun! Try to coordinate the decorations with the fashions being presented. If it is necessary to change decorations during the show, be ready to practice this during the dress rehearsal.

4. Schritt Die Generalprobe

It's almost time for the real thing, but first a dress rehearsal. There are many things to check out. Can the models present their fashions with the decorations in place? Are the fashions wearable? Is the music ready? Here's an opportunity to hear and improve your performance. Videotape or tape-record the rehearsal so that the master of ceremonies, models, and announcers hear their German. There's nothing like hearing and seeing yourself to know what you've got down pat and what needs a little more practice.

F Los, auf den Laufsteg!

When you're preparing for a show, it seems as if the show will never happen. There are only more and more things to do, but **der große Tag ist endlich da!**

Brauchbares

- German-English dictionary
- All the materials you made and gathered for the fashion show
- Worksheet folder

1. Schritt Ist alles fertig? Sind wir startbereit?

As a class, make the final preparations for your show. Arrange the decorations and the furniture. Set out the programs. Make sure the music is ready and get into your designer clothes. Have copies of your speeches handy in case you need them. If you have more than one task, make sure everything is laid out so you can easily move from one to the other.

2. Schritt Macht die Türen auf!

If you have guests, seat them and hand out the programs. Ready, set, music! Enjoy the show!

Nützliche Vokabeln

Hals- und Beinbruch!	*Break a leg!*
Was für ein schicker Pulli!	*What a stylish sweater!*
Oh, das ist echt stark!	*Wow, that is so great, terrific!*
...altmodisch	*...old-fashioned*
...hässlich [wunderschön]	*...ugly [gorgeous]*
stehen + *dative* (*used with clothing*)	*to look good on someone*
[Der Mantel] steht ihm/ihr gut.	*The coat looks good on him/her.*
passen + *dative*	*to fit someone*
[Die Hose] passt ihm/ihr nicht.	*The pants don't fit him/her.*

3. Schritt **Publikumsreaktionen**

During a fashion show, the audience often comments on what they like and dislike. If you're part of the audience, you need to be able to express and exchange your opinions. Use some of the following questions to help you discuss the clothing at the fashion show.

- Wie findest du [die Krawatte]? Wie gefällt dir [die Hose]?
- Welches Kleid magst du lieber: das blaue oder das schwarze?
- Würdest du dir so einen Hut kaufen? — Ja, schon. / Ich nie!

Noch etwas dazu

Take notes at the fashion show to expand into a newspaper review. Use what you have gathered throughout the project to help you. Pay attention to items such as these:

1. Welches war dein Lieblingskleidungsstück in der Modenschau? Warum?
2. Was hat dir nicht so gut gefallen? Warum nicht?
3. Was hältst du von den verschiedenen Kollektionen?
4. Was war für dich das Beste an dieser Modenschau?
5. Welche Aspekte von der Modenschau haben dich besonders interessiert?

PROJECT

8

Und jetzt zum Wetterbericht ...

Have you ever wanted to control the weather? Well, here's your chance! Using your knowledge of weather and German, you and your group will create a local cable news weather report for German-speaking visitors to the U.S. You can present it live or on videotape. In the process, you will:

- Collect ideas from weather reports that you watch and read
- Write a local weather forecast covering several days and give temperatures in Celsius
- Create a weather map and other illustrations to accompany your forecast
- Stage a live, on-the-scene weather report
- Rehearse and present your weather forecast

Und nun zu den Vorhersagen!

Verknüpfungen

In the process of making a weather report, you'll sharpen your skills in many areas.

- ☑ Geographie
- ☐ Geschichte
- ☐ Gesundheit und Ernährung
- ☑ Kunst
- ☑ Lernmethoden
- ☑ Mathematik
- ☑ Medien
- ☐ Musik
- ☑ Naturwissenschaft
- ☑ Technik

Look for the **Verknüpfungen** boxes throughout this project.

Warm-up: Klima und Wetter

Brauchbares

- Climate and Weather Expressions Worksheet 8.W
- Map of the U.S.
- Portfolio (binder with pockets, a file jacket, or a file folder) for each student
- The World Wide Web

A. Are you a person who is fascinated by the weather and follows forecasts closely? Or do you prefer to be surprised by the weather? As a class, brainstorm in English the times when the weather is important to you. List your ideas on the board.

B. You know what your local climate is like, and you already know some weather expressions in German. As a class, brainstorm the German expressions you know. Record them on your Climate and Weather Expressions Worksheet 8.W under Expressions I Know. Then think of other words and expressions in English that you could use to describe your local weather. List them under Expressions I May Need.

C. As a class, discuss any special or unusual facts or characteristics of your local climate and weather in English. Record them on Climate and Weather Expressions Worksheet 8.W. File your worksheet in your portfolio for later use.

D. Now think about the ways in which weather affects your daily life. In a small group, brainstorm in German the kinds of clothing you wear and the activities you do in different types of weather. Share your ideas with the class, and add to your list any new information you get from your classmates.

Hast du das gewusst?

Located in the center of Europe, Germany is about half the size of Texas (223,033 square miles, or 357,020 square kilometers). While Germany is situated further north than the United States, German weather is unusual in that the winters are not necessarily colder in the northern part of the country. The influence of the North Sea makes for a warmer and rainier winter in the northwest, while snow and frost occur more often in the regions bordering on the Baltic Sea. The south experiences snowy winters, making the Alps a popular destination for skiers and snowboarders.

E. Collect a few weather forecasts from your local newspaper and store them in your portfolio for later use.

Suchen wir im Web!

You can find information about the weather in the U.S. and the world via the World Wide Web. A great variety of information is available on-line—maps showing entire countries and regions, satellite photos, three- to five-day forecasts, and details that are only a few hours old and are updated as often as every three to six hours. Using your preferred search engine, locate several forecasts for your local area on the Web.

Keywords

news
weather
"weather [+ name of area researching]"

A Die Wettervorhersage in den Medien

Weather reports can range from simple statements of the temperature and local conditions to elaborate forecasts that give the long-term outlook and show weather patterns around the country or even the world. As you prepare to give your weather broadcast, gather some ideas from weather reports you watch on TV and read in the newspaper.

Brauchbares

- Televised weather report
- VCR
- What's in a Weather Report? Worksheet 8.A.1
- Weather maps from newspapers or the World Wide Web
- Weather Symbols Worksheet 8.A.2

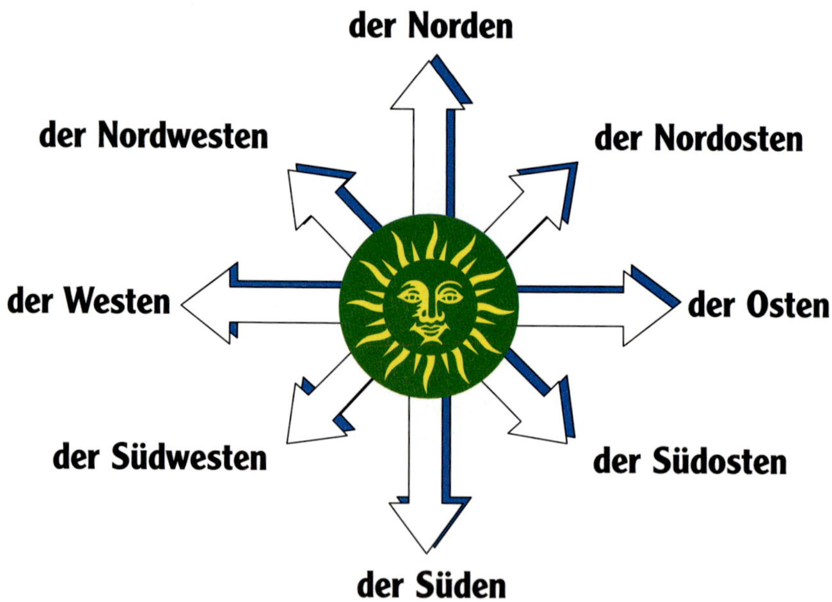

Verknüpfungen

- ☑ Geographie
- ☑ Kunst
- ☑ Medien
- ☑ Naturwissenschaft
- ☑ Technik

1. Schritt Der Wetterbericht für eure Gegend

A. What kinds of information are given in a weather report? Watch one or two on television. If possible, record one so you can look at it a few times as you collect ideas. Fill out Part 1 of What's in a Weather Report? Worksheet 8.A.1.

B. In your small group, compare in English what you recorded on your worksheets. Then talk about which features of the weather reports you might like to include in your own broadcast. Fill out Part 2 of the worksheet together. Don't worry about details at this point; just gather some ideas that you can develop in the next part of the project.

2. Schritt Wie sagt man das auf Deutsch?

A. In your small group, choose two or three different weather maps that members have collected. As you look at each one, see how much you can say about the weather in German. Use the vocabulary and expressions you've gathered on Worksheet 8.A.1 for help. If you use any German expressions that aren't already listed, jot them down. If there's an expression you don't know but want to use, look it up in the list of weather expressions in the Almanac or in a dictionary, and add it to your list.

B. As a class, discuss which expressions are proving most helpful. Be sure to add any new information to Worksheet 8.A.1.

Hast du das gewusst?

German has a number of sayings that use the weather to make a point. For instance, if someone looks sad or grumpy, people might comment: **"Du machst ein Gesicht wie sieben Tage Regenwetter"** (*Your face looks as if we've had seven days of rain*). Or if a friend lets you down in a difficult situation, you could say, **"Sie hat mich im Regen stehen lassen"** (*She left me standing in the rain*). Finally, a third saying warns you not to over-interpret the first sign of a hopeful change. So if you got one good grade after doing poorly in class, a teacher might warn, **"Eine Schwalbe macht noch keinen Sommer"** (*Seeing one swallow doesn't mean it's summer*).

3. Schritt Die meteorologischen Symbole

Weather reports in newspapers and on television generally use symbols to provide a quick visual overview of the weather. In your small group, look again at the weather maps you've collected, and gather some ideas for weather symbols you might want to use in your weather report. Add them in Column 1 of Weather Symbols Worksheet 8.A.2. Do you have other ideas for weather symbols? Draw them as well. In Column 2, write in German what each symbol stands for. Consult your dictionary or the weather expressions in the Almanac for help. When you're done, add your worksheets to your portfolio.

Suchen wir im Web!

The Web site of the National Weather Service provides a good deal of information about U.S. weather in the past, present, or future. It also provides definitions of weather symbols. Follow the path: "national weather service," weather maps, chart reference guide.

B Schreibt eure eigene Wettervorhersage!

Now that you've gathered some general ideas and information for your weather report, it's time for the details.

Brauchbares

- Worksheets 8.A.1 and 8.B
- Newspaper weather reports from different times of the year
- Almanacs with information about average annual temperatures

1. Schritt Wie fängt die Wettervorhersage an?

How do you want to begin your weather report in German? With your small group, look at the ideas you recorded on What's in a Weather Report? Worksheet 8.A.1 as well as the possibilities given below. Write a short introduction to your weather report on Weather Report Decision Worksheet 8.B. Have the news anchor introduce the forecaster. Then have the forecaster say "hello" and state the place, the day, and the date.

▶ Und jetzt die Wettervorhersage mit Roland Braun.
Guten Abend, meine Damen und Herren.
Hier ist die Wettervorhersage für Milwaukee, Wisconsin,
für Montag, den 25. Mai.

2. Schritt Wie ist das Wetter heute?

Verknüpfungen

- ☑ Geographie
- ☑ Mathematik
- ☑ Naturwissenschaft
- ☑ Technik

With your small group, choose the day of the year when your weather report will be broadcast. What's the local weather usually like at that time of year? If possible, check a newspaper weather report for the time of year you've chosen, or use an almanac to find information about average temperatures, Then decide what the weather will be like on the day of your broadcast. On Worksheet 8.B, write in German: the date you've chosen, the high and low temperatures in degrees Fahrenheit, and at least five weather expressions in German to describe the current local weather for the day you've chosen.

3. Schritt Wie misst man die Temperatur?

As you may know, most U.S. weather maps use the Fahrenheit scale to report temperatures. Your German-speaking viewers will understand your weather report better if you give the temperatures in degrees Celsius (C). Use the Fahrenheit and Celsius Conversion Chart in the weather section of the Almanac to learn how to change temperatures from one scale to another. Convert the temperatures you provided in the **2. Schritt** from Fahrenheit to Celsius. Check your results with your group and record them on Weather Report Decision Worksheet 8.B. From now on, give all your temperatures in Celsius!

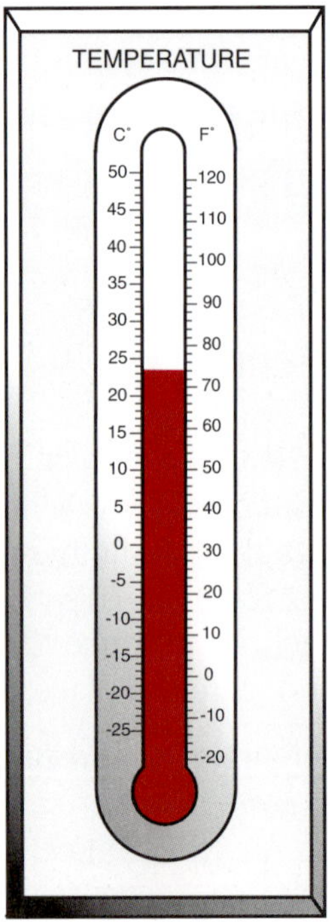

4. Schritt Das Wetter in den nächsten Tagen

A. What's the weather outlook for the next day? Your group's forecast should include some change in the weather. Write your ideas on Weather Report Decision Worksheet 8.B, and include at least five weather expressions.

B. An extended weather forecast (**die Wettervorhersage**) usually outlines the weather and temperatures for the next three to seven days. On Weather Report Decision Worksheet 8.B, write a short statement in German describing the general weather trends for the next three days.

Noch etwas dazu

Find out the times of the sunrise and sunset for the time of year you're covering in your weather report. If you live near a coast, include the times of the high and low tides as well.

Nützliche Vokabeln

Es ist neblig, bewölkt.	*It's [foggy/misty, cloudy].*
In den Alpen kann es zu Schneefall kommen.	*There's a chance of snow in the Alps.*
Die Tiefsttemperatur/ Die Höchsttemperatur liegt bei [20°C].	*The low/high temperature will be [20°C].*
Die Tiefsttemperatur/ Die Höchsttemperatur lag bei [20°C].	*The low/high temperature was [20°C].*
Sonnenaufgang ist um [7 Uhr 20].	*Sunrise is at [7:20* A.M.*].*
Sonnenuntergang ist um [19 Uhr 37].	*Sunset is at [7:37* P.M.*].*
Flut/Ebbe ist um [6 Uhr 24].	*High/low tide is at [6:24* A.M.*].*

Hast du das gewusst?

Like the Farmer's Almanac in North America, there are many **Bauernregeln** (*country sayings*) in Germany that try to predict the weather. For example, flowers and vegetables should not be planted outdoors until after the middle of May. This is because **Die Eisheiligen** (*The Holy Icy Ones*) are likely to "visit" between May 11 and 15 and bring night frost. Another **Bauernregel** uses the weather on June 27, **Siebenschläfertag** (*Dormouse Day*), to predict what the summer will be like. **"Wenn die Siebenschläfer Regen kochen, regnet's vier bis sieben Wochen"** (*When the dormice cook up rain, it will rain for four to seven weeks*). Scientifically, the accuracy of this saying is difficult to prove, but often the weather at the end of June in Germany does foreshadow what the rest of the summer will be like.

C Illustrieren wir das Wetter!

From simple illustrations to advanced radar maps and satellite pictures, visual aids are an important part of a television weather report. They can help us to understand weather patterns or give us a quick overview of the most important weather information. A weather forecaster (**der Meteorologe/die Meteorologin**) can also use maps and pictures for guidance during the weather report.

Brauchbares

- What's in a Weather Report? Worksheet 8.A.1
- Weather Symbols Worksheet 8.A.2
- Weather Report Decision Worksheet 8.B
- Poster board or foam core
- Colored markers, removable tape, index cards

1. Schritt Eure Ideen

How can you illustrate the weather in your televised weather report? Before you look at the ideas in the following steps, review the ones you collected on What's in a Weather Report? Worksheet 8.A.1. In your small group, choose an idea you think would work well and discuss what you need to do to carry it out. Make a list of any materials you need, and divide the work among the members of your group.

2. Schritt Die Wetterkarte

A weather map (**die Wetterkarte**) is a basic part of most televised weather reports. Your group is going to create one with removable weather symbols, so you can show changes in the weather over a period of time. If you're giving your weather report live, you'll need to create a map large enough to be seen easily by your audience. If you're videotaping your broadcast, you can feature close-ups of a smaller map.

Verknüpfungen

- ✔ Geographie
- ✔ Kunst
- ✔ Lernmethoden
- ✔ Naturwissenschaft

A. With your small group, locate a map of your state or region to use as a model for your weather map. On poster board, foam core, or another sturdy material, draw the basic outline of your forecast area. Add your town and a few other important towns and landmarks.

B. Now make some symbols to illustrate the weather you've described on Worksheet 8.B. Look at Worksheet 8.A.2 for ideas about how to represent the weather. On poster board, draw, color, and cut out the symbols you need. To attach them to your map during the forecast, you can use removable tape.

C. Finally, create removable labels that you can attach to the map to show each temperature and day of the week you're illustrating. On blank index cards or pieces of poster board, write each temperature in degrees Celsius and each day of the forecast in German. Attach the labels to your map with removable tape.

3. Schritt Macht eure Wettervorhersage anschaulich!

Now give an illustrated long-term forecast. On a piece of poster board, draw a row of pictures illustrating the general weather conditions for each day of the long-term forecast you outlined on Weather Report Decision Worksheet 8.B. Include the high and low temperatures as well.

Hast du das gewusst?

Most noticeable in late winter and early spring, the **Föhn** is a warm, dry wind that affects certain Alpine valleys (in Germany, Austria, and Switzerland), especially those running from south to north. It can melt snow very quickly and trigger avalanches at higher elevations. Temperatures can rise as much as 27°–36°F (15°–20°C) with the onset of a **Föhn** wind. During the **Föhn**, road accidents and acts of violence increase and some people experience headaches, depression, and abnormally aggressive urges.

D Ein Sonderbericht

Weather reports sometimes go beyond merely describing the local and regional weather. When there are important weather-related events, on-the-scene reports help viewers understand the true impact of the weather. Visitors to your area will appreciate hearing about local events and activities affected by the weather.

Brauchbares

- What's in a Weather Report? Worksheet 8.A.1
- Props for staging a live report

1. Schritt Wie ist die Vorhersage?

With your small group, decide what kind of weather you want to show in your on-the-scene report: a snowstorm? a very cold or windy day? a heat wave? a thunderstorm or hurricane? Brainstorm ideas for staging your weather scene. For example, a fan can be used to create the effect of a strong wind; a shivering reporter dressed in a heavy parka can show how cold it is; or lights turned on and off can depict lightning. Use your imagination!

2. Schritt Ein Live-Bericht

Write a short script in German for your on-the-scene reporter. Describe the weather and what it feels like to be there. Include some interviews with passersby as well. What do they think about the weather—rain for five straight days or three feet of snow? How do they feel? How do they stay warm or keep cool? How are they dressed? What are they planning to do in this weather?

Verknüpfungen

- ☑ Kunst
- ☑ Naturwissenschaft
- ☑ Technik

Nützliche Vokabeln

Wie finden Sie das Wetter heute?	*What do you think of today's weather?*
Es ist herrlich!	*It's marvelous!*
Es ist ein wunderschöner Tag.	*It's a beautiful day.*
Es geht mir auf die Nerven.	*It gets on my nerves.*
Man kann es nicht ändern.	*It can't be changed.*

3. Schritt Sonst noch was?

Look at the features you listed in Part 1 of Worksheet 8.A.1. Think of other features you'd like to add to your weather report. With your group, draw up a plan and divide the work.

Noch etwas dazu

Create a commercial for a weather-related product (umbrellas, ski resorts, air conditioners, and so on) to be broadcast during your weather report.

Hast du das gewusst?

On the third Monday of April, Zurich, Switzerland, celebrates **Sechseläuten**, a local **Frühlingsfest** (*spring holiday*). It centers around the **Böögg**, a large snowman made of cotton and filled with firecrackers, which symbolizes winter. The **Böögg** is carried in a festive parade to a large round city plaza and raised high upon a pedestal. At exactly 6 P.M., the **Böögg** is lit, horses run around it, and spectators await the snowman's explosion. It is believed that the longer it takes for the **Böögg** to explode, the longer and colder the following winter will be.

E Die Wettervorhersage geht auf Sendung!

It's almost airtime. How are all the parts of your weather broadcast going to fit together? It's time to put the final touches on your work.

Brauchbares

- All materials created for the weather report
- Equipment to videotape the weather report

1. Schritt Bereitet euch vor!

With your group, make the following important decisions. Be sure to record them.

1. In what order are you going to present the different parts of your weather report? Make an outline, leaving a couple of lines free between items for additional notes.
2. Which group member will present each part of the weather report and special features? Record this information on your outline, and make sure that each person has a script for his or her part.
3. Are you going to give your weather report live or record it on videotape? If you videotape it, decide who will record each part. Add this information to your outline.
4. How are you going to change scenes and set up and use maps and other props? Videotaping will give you more flexibility in your performance, since you can record your report in parts and stop the camera at any point to set up a new scene. If you're performing live, make sure you know who's responsible for setting up materials and helping the presenters in each part of your report. Add this information to your outline.

Verknüpfungen

- ☑ Lernmethoden
- ☑ Medien

2. Schritt Übt euren Kommentar

The key to a good performance is practice. Rehearse individually and as a group, using your maps, pictures, and other props. Have someone in your group coach you as you practice. Remember that your visual aids can help guide you through your weather report. Simply pointing to different symbols can remind you of what you want to say.

3. Schritt Die Meteorologen haben das Wort

Now, it's time for the evening news and the weather report! Flip the channels and compare weather forecasts!

4. Schritt Wer hat Recht?

So which forecast is accurate? You decide! You'll find out tomorrow!

Hast du das gewusst?

In the German-speaking countries, people are keenly aware of the effect that weather has on physical and mental health. Asthmatics and others with respiratory problems often seek out the air of **Luftkurorte** (*high altitude health spas*) such as Davos and St. Moritz in Switzerland for healing. People often comment on drafts (**Es zieht hier ja fürchterlich!** *There's a terrible draft in here!*) and blame drafts for weakening the immune system and bringing on colds and other ills. The **Föhn**, that unpredictable warm, dry Alpine wind, also causes headaches and uncomfortable mood changes in some people.

PROJECT

9

Bleib gesund!

In this project your class will set up and run a health center. Its purpose will be to help educate German-speaking clients about the benefits of a healthy lifestyle and how to maintain their health through nutrition, exercise, and so on. Working with a group of your classmates, you'll accomplish the following tasks along the way:

- Complete and label a drawing of the human body
- Research good nutrition and make a food pyramid
- Create a chart illustrating the health benefits of physical activity
- Design forms to be used by clients and health counselors
- Create a brochure to advertise your health center
- Set up and run your health center

Gesundheit!

Verknüpfungen

In the process of opening a health center, you'll sharpen your skills in many areas.

- [ ] Geographie
- [ ] Geschichte
- [x] Gesundheit und Ernährung
- [x] Kunst
- [x] Lernmethoden
- [ ] Mathematik
- [ ] Medien
- [ ] Musik
- [x] Naturwissenschaft
- [x] Technik

Look for the **Verknüpfungen** boxes throughout this project.

Warm-up: Gesund leben

Brauchbares

- Newspapers and magazines
- Cardboard, poster board, or construction paper
- Tape, string, or stapler

1. Schritt Bildmaterial suchen

Working in your group, search magazines and newspapers to find pictures that you associate with good health. They might include pictures of athletes, people exercising, or healthy foods, to give you just a few ideas. Gather a variety of images.

2. Schritt Eine Collage zusammenstellen

A. With your group, arrange the pictures you've found into a colorful collage showing many different images of health. Label as many of the pictures as possible with words and descriptive captions in German.

B. Look at some of the other collages in your class to see how many different ideas, activities, and topics are associated with the word *health*. Then, have a short class discussion about what you've discovered.

3. Schritt Eine Gesundheitsmappe führen

At the end of each section in this unit, you'll need to save what you've made and learned for use later in your health center. To organize this material, your group needs to make a large portfolio. (It should be about 2 feet x 3 feet when closed.) You can do this by tying, taping, or stapling together two large pieces of cardboard, poster board, or construction paper. Attaching a handle will make your portfolio easier to carry. Label your folder **Gesundheitsmappe** (*health resources folder*).

Hast du das gewusst?

In German-speaking countries, spending up to four weeks at a health resort (**Kurort**) is quite affordable. In fact, these stays are usually paid for by health insurance! **Kurorten**, often located in areas with thermal springs, offer a series of health treatments for people at risk for or currently suffering from serious chronic ailments. While a **Kur** is definitely a nice long vacation, it is also a regimen of daily treatments. Depending on the medical situation, people may take mud baths, gargle with thermal water, see a doctor daily, and undergo physical therapy (**Krankengymnastik**). They also may learn about correct eating habits and mind and body relaxation.

A Der menschliche Körper

An important resource in a health facility is an illustration of the human body. It's used to illustrate the bones, muscles, and systems of the body, such as how blood flows through the body or how food is digested.

Brauchbares

- German-English dictionary
- Encyclopedia or anatomy book
- Colored markers
- Human Body Worksheet 9.A
- Health resources folder

1. Schritt Die verschiedenen Körperteile

On Human Body Worksheet 9.A, give German names for the parts of the body that can be seen by looking at a person, such as nose, ears, arms, and toes. Before you consult your textbook or a dictionary, see how many you can come up with on your own!

2. Schritt Die inneren Organe

A. With your group, find an illustration of the human body's internal organs, such as the heart, lungs, and stomach, in an encyclopedia or anatomy book. Make a list of eight major internal organs to add to the illustration on Human Body Worksheet 9.A. Then find their German names and write them down as well.

B. Draw the basic forms of eight internal organs on the illustration on Human Body Worksheet 9.A. Refer to the illustration in the encyclopedia or anatomy book to be sure you locate them properly in the body. Finally, use colored markers to label the organs.

Verknüpfungen

- ✔ Lernmethoden
- ✔ Naturwissenschaft

3. Schritt Die Gesundheitsmappe ergänzen

Add completed Human Body Worksheet 9.A to your health resources folder for later use.

Hast du das gewusst?

Many people in the German-speaking countries combine sports with socializing by joining a **Turnverein** (*local sports club*). Even though **Turnen** (*gymnastics*) is still the core activity of these clubs, a **Turnverein** usually offers a variety of team and individual sports, from **Fußball** (*soccer*) and **Leichtathletik** (*track and field*) to **Gymnastik** (*stretching and general fitness*) and **Ballett** (*ballet*). People often join a **Turnverein** at a very young age and stay lifelong members. Very active teams regularly compete against other teams from the same region in **Wettkämpfe** (*tournaments*).

B Die richtige Ernährung

Proper eating habits are necessary for a healthy lifestyle. One function of a health center is educating clients about good nutrition. You may be surprised by how much you already know about eating sensibly!

Brauchbares

- Encyclopedia, health or science textbooks, books about health and nutrition
- German-English dictionary
- Colored markers or computer-drawing software, poster board, paper
- Nutrition Worksheet 9.B
- Health resources folder

1. Schritt — Eine Liste mit Lebensmitteln

In your group, brainstorm in German a list of as many different foods as you can without using a dictionary. Refer to the food vocabulary in the Almanac to get started. You may be surprised at how much you know! When your list is ready, share it with another group in your class, and expand your list with ideas from the other group.

2. Schritt — Die Ernährungspyramide

Verknüpfungen

- ✔ Gesundheit und Ernährung
- ✔ Kunst
- ✔ Naturwissenschaft
- ✔ Technik

A. Nutritionists, people who study how the body uses different foods, have developed the food pyramid as a guide for sensible eating. It shows what people should eat to get the right amount of each food group. Look at the food pyramid in the Warm-up section. Then write the different types of food in German on the pyramid in Part 1 of Nutrition Worksheet 9.B. Now record the foods you listed in the **1. Schritt** in the correct section of the food pyramid. Where would you list **grüne Bohnen**, for example? Or what about **Joghurt?**

B. What is good nutrition? In your group, discuss in English what you know about the food pyramid and good nutrition. Then use colored markers or a computer with drawing software to draw a large food pyramid on poster board or a large piece of paper. Label each part of the pyramid with the German name for the type of food that belongs there. Using the list your group created in the **1. Schritt**, draw foods in each category on your pyramid and label them in German. Display your food pyramid in the health center.

3. Schritt Regeln für eine gesunde Ernährung

The bottom level of the food pyramid is the largest, showing that such foods should be eaten the most. The foods on the top level should be eaten in the smallest quantities. Using your food pyramid, create a list of four rules for healthy eating. Record your rules for proper nutrition in Part 2 of Nutrition Worksheet 9.B. Add your food pyramid and Nutrition Worksheet 9.B to your health resources folder.

Nützliche Vokabeln

Man sollte [+ *infinitive*].	*You/One should ___.*
Man muss [+ *infinitive*].	*You/One must ___.*
Ich empfehle dir [Obst] zu [essen].	*I suggest that you [eat] [fruit].*
Sie sollten/Du solltest ___ essen/trinken.	*You should eat/drink ___.*

Hast du das gewusst?

In German, there are several colorful figures of speech that refer to the human body. For example, if you are determined to stay unimpressed by someone's pleading, you would say **"Und wenn du dich auf den Kopf stellst und mit den Beinen wackelst"** (*And even if you stand on your head!*). To wish someone good luck, you would say "**Hals- und Beinbruch**!" (*Break a leg!*). Finally, after a good, hard laugh, you could say "**Ich habe mir vor Lachen den Bauch gehalten**" (*I split my sides laughing*).

C Körperliche Bewegung

Physical activity and exercise are necessary for overall well-being. Your health center will give visitors information about how proper exercise can improve their health.

Brauchbares

- Encyclopedia and books about health
- Exercise Worksheet 9.C
- Nutrition Worksheet 9.B
- Health resources folder

1. Schritt — Fitnesstraining

A. There are many different ways to get exercise. On your own, list in German five of your favorite free-time activities (**Freizeitbeschäftigungen**) that use physical energy. Write them down in Part 1, column 1, on Exercise Worksheet 9.C. For ideas, refer to the list of sports in the Almanac.

▶ eine Fahrradtour machen (*to go bike riding*)

B. Continue on your own on the same worksheet. In Part 2, column 1, under **Alltagsbeschäftigungen** (*Everyday activities*), write the names of three everyday activities or chores that you think take enough energy to offer health benefits.

▶ den Rasen mähen (*mowing the lawn*)

Verknüpfungen

- ✔ Gesundheit und Ernährung
- ✔ Naturwissenschaft
- ✔ Lernmethoden

2. Schritt Was wird dabei trainiert?

A. What are the health benefits of all eight activities you've listed? Decide which part(s) of the body are exercised during each activity. Record one on Exercise Worksheet 9.C in column 2 under **Körperteile und Organe.**

▶ eine Fahrradtour machen	das Herz
den Rasen mähen	die Beine

B. In your group, use the phrases below to compare your lists of exercises, activities, and health benefits. Come up with a list of four suggestions for getting exercise, and write them in Part 3 of Exercise Worksheet 9.C for use in your health center.

Nützliche Vokabeln

Ich habe ___ gern.	*I like to ___.*
Das ist gut für ___.	*It's good for ___.*

Noch etwas dazu

Use some of the materials listed in the **Brauchbares** box to find out how many calories are burned during each activity you've listed. Remember to include how long you must perform the activity to use that number of calories. Add this information to Exercise Worksheet 9.C in column 3, under **Kalorienverbrauch pro Trainingseinheit**. Add the worksheet to your health resources folder.

D Ein Fragebogen

Your health center will communicate with clients in various ways. You'll talk on the phone with them, interview them in person, and educate them with the charts and pictures you've made. But first you'll need to get some basic information from your clients by using a standard form that they will fill out when they visit the center. Such information will be used by doctors, nurses, counselors, the billing department, and so on.

Brauchbares

- Computer with a word-processing program
- German-English dictionary
- Health resources folder

1. Schritt — Fragen aussuchen

As a class, brainstorm a list of questions in German that a receptionist at a health center might ask to gather information about clients. Come up with at least five useful questions. Go over the questions to make sure you haven't forgotten anything important. Write the questions on the board.

2. Schritt — Das Formblatt entwerfen

In your group, organize the information you brainstormed into a German-language form. You might want to design it on the computer. Be sure to include blanks for the visitors to fill out and a space for the health counselor's comments. Since group members will take turns playing different roles, be sure to make multiple copies. Add the forms to your health resources folder for use in Section F.

Verknüpfungen

- ☑ Gesundheit und Ernährung
- ☑ Technik

E Eine Broschüre

In order to attract clients, it's important to advertise the services available at your health center. One of the best ways to do this is by making a brochure to distribute to the public.

Brauchbares

- Computer with a word-processing program
- Health resources folder
- The local telephone book with yellow pages

1. Schritt Die Geschäftsordnung

A. Working in your small group, come up with a creative idea for a German name for your health center. It may be helpful to review the information in your health resources folder. Consider practical names (**Zentrum für Fitness und Ernährung**) and clever ones (**Der Jungbrunnen**). Present your ideas to your class, and together choose one to be the name of your center. All of the groups will be working together in the center, so you need only one name.

B. As a class, decide on the schedule of your center. Will it be open only on weekdays? Will it operate any evenings in order to accommodate clients' school and work schedules? Come up with a list of hours (**die Öffnungszeiten**) to include in your brochure. Remember to start with **Montag** as the first day of the week. Since you're making a schedule, use a 24-hour clock—1:00 P.M. is **13 Uhr**, 2:00 P.M. is **14 Uhr**, and so forth.

C. Next, decide what general information about your health center will need to be included in your brochure. Brainstorm this information in English, while your teacher lists it on the board. Remember to include the basic details about your center (name, address, and so on) as well as a description of its function, services, and so forth. Will you include any drawings or photos?

Verknüpfungen

- ✔ Lernmethoden
- ✔ Technik

DER JUNGBRUNNEN

Apfelweg 36

70176 Stuttgart

Tel. (0711) 6 45 99

2. Schritt Wer macht was?

Divide the information you listed on the board among the small groups in your class. Each group will be responsible for creating one section of the informative brochure about your health center (for example, A. Our Mission, B. Nutrition Courses, and so forth). Remember that you may need to invent some of the information, such as the German-language address, phone number, and so on. A word processor may make the brochure look more professional. Use the resources in the **Brauchbares** box to help you, and be creative!

3. Schritt Die Broschüre wird zusammengestellt

When all the groups are finished, put your brochure together. Make multiple copies or ask your teacher to photocopy it for you. Put your brochures in your health resources folder.

Noch etwas dazu

Design business cards for your health center.

F Der Tag der Eröffnung

Your health center is nearly ready to open. There are just a few final preparations to be made. When everything is ready, open the center.

Brauchbares

- Completed health resources folder, including worksheets 9.B and 9.C, food pyramids, brochures
- Poster board and colored markers
- German-English dictionary

1. Schritt Die letzten Vorbereitungen

A. Choose one group to make a sign in German for the outside of your center. Post the name of the center and the days and hours it's open to the public.

B. Another group in your class should make smaller signs for the different departments of the center such as the reception area, waiting room, and counselors. Make your signs in German, of course!

WARTEZIMMER
(waiting room)

EMPFANG
(RECEPTION DESK)

Gesundheitsberater
(counselors)

Verknüpfungen

- ✔ Gesundheit und Ernährung
- ✔ Kunst

c. Meanwhile, the remaining groups should set up the classroom for use as a health center. Chairs need to be placed in the waiting room, desks arranged for the receptionists and health counselors, and so on. Hang the collages and drawings of the human body and food pyramids in appropriate places in the classroom for use in the center. Finally, post the signs that the groups have created and put the brochures on display.

2. Schritt Fertig?

Within each group, decide who will play the roles of receptionists, health counselors, and clients at the center.

Receptionists (**die Mitarbeiter am Empfang**) need pens and the forms you created. Health counselors (**die Gesundheitsberater**) should take the remaining health resources from the health resources folders and sit at the desks placed in the counseling area to wait for clients. Clients (**die Kunden**) should decide on at least two questions to ask the health counselors, along with the reason for their visit to the center. Is it to learn about health in general? To learn new exercises? To get nutritional information? Jot this information down in German.

3. Schritt Zu Ihren Diensten!

Your health center is open. Clients enter, talk with receptionists, and fill out forms. A few clients call the center to inquire about hours and receptionists answer.

▶ Guten Morgen/Guten Tag. Hier [*name of center*].

Some receptionists can sit near the door of the classroom, handing out forms. Others answer phones. Still others receive completed forms and direct clients to the health counselors.

Health counselors ask clients how they feel and what they want to learn at the center. Using information from the food pyramid and from Nutrition Worksheet 9.B and Exercise Worksheet 9.C, counselors should suggest nutrition and exercise options to clients. After talking with a counselor, clients may then become receptionists or counselors, so that everyone gets to play more than one role. Be creative!

Nützliche Vokabeln

Die Mitarbeiter am Empfang:	*Receptionists:*
Wie kann ich Ihnen helfen?	*How may I help you?*
Bitte füllen Sie dieses Formular aus.	*Please fill out this form.*
Die Kunden:	*Clients:*
Was soll ich hier hinschreiben?	*What should I write here?*
Wie lange muss ich warten, bis ich mit einem Gesundheitsberater sprechen kann?	*How long do I have to wait to speak to a counselor?*
Ich habe einen Termin mit einem Gesundheitsberater.	*I have an appointment to see a counselor.*
Ich fühle mich [müde, schlecht, gestresst, usw.].	*I feel [tired, bad, stressed, etc.].*
Welche Übungen sind gut für den/die/das [*part of body*]?	*Which exercises are good for the [part of the body]?*
Welche Lebensmittel sind gesund?	*Which foods are healthy?*
Ich hätte gerne Informationen zu ___.	*I'd like information about ___.*
Die Gesundheitsberater:	*Health counselors:*
Was möchten Sie wissen?	*What would you like to know?*
[Schwimmen] ist sehr gut für die Muskeln.	*[Swimming] is great for the muscles.*

PROJECT

10

Eröffnen wir eine Gaststätte!

Using your knowledge of the foods and cultures of German-speaking countries, you and your group will open your own restaurant. In the process you will:

- Choose a type of restaurant and a name
- Decide on a location
- Decide on your restaurant's specialties
- Devise a decorating scheme and select background music
- Hire staff
- Design your menu
- Advertise your restaurant
- Prepare a shopping list of the foods you need to make your menu items

On opening day, you will set up your restaurant in the classroom, greet customers, seat them, take their orders, and enjoy your food.

Guten Appetit!

Verknüpfungen

In the process of opening a restaurant, you will sharpen your skills in many areas.

- ✔ Geographie
- ✔ Geschichte
- ✔ Gesundheit und Ernährung
- ✔ Kunst
- ✔ Lernmethoden
- ✔ Mathematik
- ✔ Medien
- ✔ Musik
- ☐ Naturwissenschaft
- ✔ Technik

Look for the **Verknüpfungen** boxes throughout this project.

Warm-up: Bitte zu Tisch!

Brauchbares

- Cookbooks and magazines with recipes from German-speaking countries
- Guidebooks for German-speaking countries
- The World Wide Web
- Folder or portfolio to store your research

A. With a small group of your classmates, discuss in German some of your favorite foods. Refer to the food vocabulary in the German Almanac.

Nützliche Vokabeln

Was isst du gern?	*What do you like to eat?*
Meine Lieblingsspeise ist ___.	*My favorite dish is ___.*

B. Now, think about any experiences you may have had with German restaurants in the U.S. Mention foods from German-speaking countries that you have tasted or have heard about. Have you tried them? Would you like to? Are they different from your favorite foods? Discuss your ideas with your group.

C. Using some of the resources listed in the **Brauchbares** box, find some information about foods or meals in a German-speaking country. Write down in German at least two interesting facts to share with your group. Then put the facts in your folder.

Suchen wir im Web!

Begin your Web search for information about foods in German-speaking countries by clicking on the Society and Culture or the Regional sections of your Web guide. Continue narrowing your search by clicking on the subsections provided, for example Food and Drink or Countries and Cultures. Finally, click on the name of a German-speaking country and then investigate the various suggested Web sites. Bookmark useful sites.

D. In your group, discuss what you have learned about foods and meals in the countries and regions you chose. Did anything surprise you? As a class, discuss any differences and similarities you have discovered between foods and mealtimes in the U.S. and in German-speaking countries.

Noch etwas dazu

As homework or in your group, make a chart showing the usual mealtimes and the typical foods eaten at each meal in the U.S. and in one or more of the German-speaking countries. The U.S. section should be in English, and the German section in German. Use the following chart as a guide.

Meal/Mahlzeit	U.S.	[German-speaking country]
breakfast/ **das Frühstück**	time: typical foods:	Uhrzeit: typische Speisen:
lunch/ **das Mittagessen**	time: typical foods:	Uhrzeit: typische Speisen:
dinner/ **das Abendessen, das Abendbrot**	time: typical foods:	Uhrzeit: typische Speisen:

A Erste Entscheidungen

When opening a restaurant, or any business, you must make many decisions—some big, some small. You are going to begin by choosing the type of restaurant you will open and deciding on a name for it.

Brauchbares

- German–English dictionary
- Business Decisions Worksheet 10.A
- Portfolio or folder for storing worksheets

1. Schritt Was für eine Gaststätte wollen wir eröffnen?

Keeping in mind what you have learned about foods and mealtimes in German-speaking countries, decide with your group what type of restaurant you would like to open. Are you interested in a café-style restaurant with outdoor seating or a fast-food restaurant for business people? a carry-out place at the beach? an after-ski coffee shop? Will your restaurant be large or small? casual or elegant?

2. Schritt Wie nennen wir unsere Gaststätte?

A. Working with your group, brainstorm a list of adjectives in German that could describe your restaurant. Use your dictionary or textbook for further inspiration.

B. Using your list of adjectives and your creativity, work with your group to invent a clever German name for your restaurant.

Verknüpfungen

☑ Lernmethoden

Mom's

Ratskeller Böblingen

Pasta Palace

Café Mozart

The Greasy Spoon

Restaurant Rheinblick

The Blue Onion

Gasthof zum Schwan

Landgasthof zur Brücke

Fred's Roadside Diner

Die Alpenrose

Fish n' Fowl

3. Schritt Wir machen einen Plan

Now that you have made two key decisions about your restaurant, ask your teacher for a copy of Business Decisions Worksheet 10.A and record these and future decisions. Put your worksheet in your portfolio (or folder) for future reference.

Hast du das gewusst?

German speakers don't buy coffee "to go" and walk around with it, as Americans do. Instead, they frequent cafés to drink a leisurely cup of coffee, watch the world go by, or meet friends. In good weather, tables are placed on sidewalks or patios (**Terrassen**), and customers may sit inside (**drinnen**) or outside (**draußen**). Cafés may also offer sandwiches, snacks, and fresh pastries. **Würstchenbuden**, stands offering many types of grilled sausages, are also popular for quick meals.

B Der ideale Standort

In opening a business, location is everything. Restaurants are often placed in or near well-populated areas to attract as much business as possible. Restaurants need to be easy for their customers to find and there needs to be a demand for them in the chosen location. For example, it makes more sense to open an exotic specialty restaurant on a busy city street than in a quiet suburb. Locating your restaurant near a busy intersection or a tourist attraction would also help bring in customers. Or perhaps you are a risk-taker and want to locate it in a lesser-known area.

Brauchbares

- Travel guides; maps of German-speaking countries and cities
- Encyclopedias, travel magazines, guidebooks
- Business Decisions Worksheet 10.A
- The World Wide Web

Verknüpfungen

- ☑ Geographie
- ☑ Kunst
- ☑ Technik

1. Schritt Welche Möglichkeiten gibt es?

A. Keeping in mind the type of restaurant you have chosen to establish, discuss the following questions in your group:

1. Wie wichtig ist die Lage (*location*) für eure Gaststätte?

   Wollt ihr eure Gaststätte lieber in der Stadt oder auf dem Lande aufmachen? am Meer oder am Fluss? in den Bergen? mitten im Wald? in der Stadtmitte?

   Wie kommen die Leute zu euch ins Restaurant? Gibt es eine Haltestelle für öffentliche Verkehrsmittel in der Nähe? Gibt es Parkplätze?

2. Welche Leute werden eure Kunden sein? Geschäftsleute? Familien? Schüler und Studenten? Touristen? Senioren?

B. Using the resources listed in the **Brauchbares** box, look for locations that fit the criteria you have established.

Suchen wir im Web!

Use the Recreation or Travel section of a Web guide to link to listings of restaurants or Web sites of restaurants in cities in German-speaking countries.

2. Schritt Eine endgültige Entscheidung treffen

A. In your group, discuss all the possible locations for your restaurant, and then decide as a group on an ideal location.

B. On Business Decisions Worksheet 10.A, write a brief description in German of your restaurant's location, including important geographical markers. Explain why you chose the location. Put the worksheet in your portfolio (or folder) for future reference.

C. As homework or in your group, draw a map of the location, labeling landmarks, geographical features, and streets (in German, of course!). Mark the exact location of your restaurant.

C Die Spezialität des Hauses

Many restaurants have a few specialty items on their menus that are their customers' favorites. Locations near a forest, for example, may feature mushroom dishes and game, such as venison and wild boar. In Switzerland, fondue (a hot dish of melted cheese that is eaten with bread) is often the featured item.

Brauchbares

- Cookbooks and food magazines
- The World Wide Web

1. Schritt Die Rezepte

Look through cookbooks and food magazines to find recipes for menu items you might want to feature in your restaurant. Put together a recipe book for dishes you want to serve.

Suchen wir im Web!

You can find recipes on the Web! Use a search engine and the keywords to the right or click the Lifestyles, Travel, or Culture sections of a Web guide. Then continue narrowing your search by clicking in appropriate sections such as Food and Drink, Recipes, or Restaurants, until you reach a list of Web sites.

Keywords

Rezept
Restaurant
Gasthof
Speisen
Gastronomie

Verknüpfungen

- ✔ Gesundheit und Ernährung
- ✔ Lernmethoden
- ✔ Mathematik
- ✔ Technik

2. Schritt Ein Geheimrezept

Work with your group to choose one item from your recipe book that you would like to feature as your house specialty. Remember to take into account the location of your restaurant and the region's specialties.

Hast du das gewusst?

Measurements for ingredients in recipes from German-speaking countries may vary from those of a typical recipe in the U.S. For example, flour is usually measured by weight (in grams) rather than by volume (in cups), and liquids are measured in liters.

Noch etwas dazu

Imagine that your group chose the recipe that follows as your restaurant's specialty. Adapt it to the quantity needed to serve your customers!

Limonade

- *12 Zitronen*
- *1,5 Liter Wasser*
- *300 Gramm Zucker*

Eiswürfel, Zitronensaft, Zucker und Wasser in eine Karaffe oder einen Krug geben. Das Ganze gut mischen. Je nach Geschmack mehr Wasser oder Zucker zugeben. Eiskalt servieren! Das Rezept ist für 6 Personen berechnet.

A. Keeping in mind the size and the clientele of your restaurant, estimate the number of people per day who will be ordering your house specialty. If your recipe serves more than one person, divide the number of servings into the number of customers per day who will order the item. The result is the number of batches of the recipe you will need to make in one day. For example, the lemonade recipe on page 181 serves six. If sixty people per day will order lemonade, then the number of pitchers of lemonade needed is ten.

B. You now need to increase the ingredient amounts in your recipe. To do this, multiply the quantity of each ingredient in your recipe by the number of batches needed. Here are the calculations for the lemonade recipe:

Limonade

10 x 12 Zitronen = 120 Zitronen

10 x 1.5 Liter Wasser = 15 Liter Wasser

10 x 300 Gramm Zucker = 3000 Gramm Zucker

Nützliche Vokabeln

mal	*multiplied by*
durch	*divided by*
macht	*equal(s)*

D Die Dekoration

The ambiance, or atmosphere, of a restaurant is established subtly through the décor of the dining room, the seating arrangement, the lighting, and the background music.

Brauchbares

- Cookbooks and food magazines
- Magazines showing decorating ideas
- Guidebooks for German-speaking countries
- Art books or pictures of artwork from German-speaking countries
- Recordings of popular, traditional, and classical music of the German-speaking countries
- Business Decisions Worksheet 10.A
- The World Wide Web and encyclopedias

Nützliche Vokabeln

anstreichen	*to paint*
die Beleuchtung	*lighting*
der Boden, -̈	*floor*
dekorieren, verzieren	*to decorate*
die Farbe, -n	*paint (for walls)*
der Holzboden, -̈	*hardwood floor*
der Kachelboden, -̈	*tile floor*
die Kerze, -n	*candle*
die Tapete, -n	*wallpaper*
tapezieren	*to wallpaper*
der Teppich, -e	*rug*
der Teppichboden, -̈	*wall-to-wall carpeting*

Verknüpfungen

- ☑ Geschichte
- ☑ Kunst
- ☑ Medien
- ☑ Musik
- ☑ Technik

1. Schritt Allgemeine Ideen

A. Keeping in mind the type of restaurant you have chosen, discuss the following questions:

1. Welche Farben möchten wir in unserer Gaststätte benutzen?
2. Was für einen Boden wollen wir? einen Holzboden? einen Teppichboden?
3. Wie soll die Beleuchtung sein? Haben wir Kerzen auf den Tischen?

B. Draw a picture of your interior decorating scheme or cut out and compile magazine photos that reflect your ideas. Label the various elements in German, using the **Nützliche Vokabeln** as a guide.

2. Schritt Bilder für die Wände!

A. As homework or in your group, consult textbooks, art books, and encyclopedias to identify four pieces of art to decorate your restaurant.

B. Present one piece of art to your group and explain in German or English why you like it and have chosen it.

Suchen wir im Web!

You can also locate information about artists and pictures of their works on the Web. If you already have an artist in mind, use his or her complete name in your Web search. You can enclose the entire name in quotes or first try the last name and then refine your search with the artist's first and middle names. You may, however, want to browse at a museum's Web site for artwork from the country in which your restaurant is located.

Keywords

name of artist
name of museum
Kunstmuseum
name of an artistic genre (e.g., impressionism)

Noch etwas dazu

Write a brief description in German of each piece of art you have chosen. Include the artist's name, the date of the work, and a brief description of the work.

3. Schritt Die Tischdekoration

Using plastic or paper plates, design the china pattern your restaurant will use. Does your design reflect the cultural heritage or a historical period of the country in which your restaurant is located? For instance, did you use a traditional **Dresdner Porzellan** pattern? Or did you design something modern, flashy, and innovative? Also choose the color and design of your napkins and place mats or tablecloths.

Noch etwas dazu

Make some sample napkins and place mats.

Hast du das gewusst?

Many restaurants in the German-speaking world share some common traits. Typically, the ceiling is made of dark wood to create a **gemütlich** (*cozy, comfortable*) atmosphere. Windows may be made of colored or opaque glass, or covered with lace curtains. Also, patrons seat themselves. If the restaurant is full, it is common to walk over to a table with empty seats, ask if they are available (**Sind diese Plätze noch frei?**), and share the table with the people already seated.

4. Schritt Passende Musik auswählen

Now it's time to choose some background music to set the right mood.

A. What do you know about the music of the areas associated with the cuisine of your restaurant? Discuss your ideas with your group.

B. There are several ways you can find out more about music from the German-speaking world. Your library may have books and recordings. Using these or other resources, find one or two musicians, music groups, or composers who interest you and share information about them with your group.

C. With your music research in hand, consider the type of restaurant you are going to open. Include its clientele, location, and menu. For instance, a restaurant in a small Swiss mountain **Dorf** (*village*) is more likely to play Alpine folk music rather than the latest Top 40 rock hits, unless it caters to students. With your group, choose some background music for your restaurant.

5. Schritt Wie haben wir uns entschieden?

Record your decisions about décor and music on Business Decisions Worksheet 10.A and file it in your portfolio (or folder).

E Das Personal

No matter how big or small your restaurant is, you need to hire a competent staff to help you run it.

Brauchbares

- Help Wanted ads from German-language newspapers
- Interview Worksheet 10.E

Nützliche Vokabeln

die Bedienung	*service; waitstaff*
der Gastwirt/die Gastwirtin	*manager, employer*
der Kassierer/die Kassiererin	*cashier*
der Kellner/die Kellnerin	*waiter/waitress*
der Koch/die Köchin	*cook*
Herr Ober/Frau Ober!	*Oh, waiter/waitress!*

Verknüpfungen

- ☑ Medien
- ☑ Technik

1. Schritt Die Angestellten und ihre Aufgaben

In your group, discuss the types of positions you need to fill (cooks or chefs, waitstaff, and so forth) in order to run your restaurant. Make a list in German of the help you will need and what their duties will be.

Noch etwas dazu

Look at some Help Wanted ads in German-language newspapers, in your textbook, or the ad below. Then write an ad for one of the positions open at your new restaurant. Be creative!

WIR SUCHEN:

KELLNER/KELLNERIN

3 Jahre Diensterfahrung.

Freundlich und zuverlässig,

auch unter Stress.

Telefon: (04138) 2 05 94

2. Schritt Vorbereitung auf das Vorstellungsgespräch

Prepare to interview potential employees. Find out each applicant's name, address, phone number, where he or she currently works, and for what position the applicant is interviewing. With your group, make a list in German of the questions you can ask to get this information.

3. Schritt Das Vorstellungsgespräch

Take turns interviewing applicants from another group in your class. Record your interview notes on Interview Worksheet 10.E. Put the worksheet in your portfolio (or folder) for future reference.

F Die Speisekarte

Choosing and creating the menu is an exciting and challenging aspect of opening a restaurant. Let your taste buds and sense of design run wild!

Brauchbares

- Cookbooks and food magazines
- Restaurant menus
- Currency exchange rate table from the newspaper, bank, or the World Wide Web (see Almanac)
- Computer with drawing-tool software
- Colored markers or pencils, paper

Nützliche Vokabeln

frisch	*fresh*
frittiert	*deep-fried*
gebacken, geröstet	*baked, roasted, grilled*
gebraten	*pan-fried*
gedünstet	*steamed*
gegrillt	*grilled*
lecker	*delicious*
mild, leicht	*mild*
paniert	*breaded*
pikant	*spicy (not hot)*
saftig	*juicy*
scharf	*spicy-hot*

Verknüpfungen

- ☑ Gesundheit und Ernährung
- ☑ Kunst
- ☑ Mathematik
- ☑ Technik

1. Schritt

Was wollen wir servieren?

In your group, use some of the resources listed in the **Brauchbares** box on page 189 and your recipe book from Section C for help in selecting at least two dishes for each category on your menu. Refer to the categories on the following menu as guides, and keep in mind the type of restaurant and location you have chosen.

Gasthof zum Brunnen

Am Brunnenplatz 127, Bergwitz
Täglich geöffnet von 11 bis 21.30 Uhr

VORSPEISEN
Lachs auf Toast $6.95
Tagessuppe: Leberknödelsuppe $4.25
Gemischter Salatteller $6.50

HAUPTGERICHTE
Rheinischer Sauerbraten mit Spätzle $16.50
Schweinebraten mit Salzkartoffeln $15.95
Paniertes Wiener Schnitzel $12.75
Scampi in Kräuterbuttersoße $16.00
Halbes Hähnchen mit Bratkartoffeln $11.75

GETRÄNKE
Mineralwasser $1.75
Limonade $2.25
Kaffee, Tee $1.25

NACHSPEISE
Rote Grütze $4.75
Frische Erdbeertorte mit Schlagsahne $5.75

(Prices in US$) (Bedienung im Preis eingeschlossen)

2. Schritt Die Preise festlegen

In order to appeal to tourists or business people from the U.S., you may want to give prices in both U.S. dollars and in the local currency (for example, **Österreichische Schilling** in Austria or euros in the EU member countries).

A. Consider how much you want to charge for your food and beverages, and assign prices in dollars to your menu items.

B. Now determine the currency of the country where your restaurant is located by consulting the monetary unit chart in the Almanac section of this book. Look up the current rate of exchange for this currency in a local or national newspaper or use the Web search guidelines supplied in the Almanac below the monetary unit chart.

C. Finally, multiply the dollar price of each of your menu items by the current exchange rate and list your menu prices in the local currency. For example, if a dollar is worth 13.30 schillings, a $2.00 cup of coffee would cost 26.60 schillings.

3. Schritt Entwerft die Speisekarte!

A. How do you want your menu to look? Before you design your own menu, look at some sample menus for layout and design ideas. Bring in a menu to discuss with your group and compare it to the ones brought in by your classmates. Describe what you like and don't like about the menus.

B. Make a menu using paper, pencils, and markers, or design it on the computer, possibly with the aid of drawing-tool software. Remember to include the various categories (first course, main course, and so on), the items within those categories, and the prices both in the appropriate foreign currency and in U.S. dollars.

Noch etwas dazu

Expand the menu by including a brief description of each item on it.

4. Schritt Möchten Sie jetzt bestellen?

Make a form that the waitstaff can use to take customers' orders. You may wish to use a simplified version of your menu, leaving space next to each item to check off customer orders. Be sure to leave some room at the bottom for the servers to total the bill.

Hast du das gewusst?

While eating customs in the German-speaking world often transcend national borders, regional specialties distinguish one region from another. Traditionally, people eat the main meal at midday (**das Mittagessen**). It usually consists of soup or an appetizer, a main course with meat, potatoes, and vegetables, and a simple dessert. Those who can go home for lunch do—most schools in Germany have no lunchrooms and students go home to eat a bigger mid-day meal. At work, many businesses have their own employee restaurant (**die Kantine**). These traditions are changing, however, as more working couples and families opt for a hot meal together in the evening at home.

In restaurants, the main dish (**das Hauptgericht**) includes potatoes, dumplings, noodles, or rice. Vegetables or a salad may or may not be included, but they can always be ordered as a side dish (**Beilage**). Rolls and butter are not necessarily included in the meal and may cost extra. If you expect a free glass of ice water with your meal, you will be disappointed—German speakers consider tap water unsavory and generally order bottled water (**Mineralwasser**).

Regional specialties in the German-speaking world vary greatly. Switzerland has made **Fondue** a household word. Near the North and Baltic seas, recipes feature fish and shrimp, while Swabians are proud of their oversized ravioli, **Maultaschen**. Cities also have their own specialties: Vienna has its plate-sized veal cutlets, **Wiener Schnitzel**, and Berlin its smoked pork chops, **Kassler Rippchen**. The Rhineland is known for sweet-and-sour roast beef, **Sauerbraten**, and Munich for shanks of pork, **Schweinshaxen**, and **Leberkäs**, a veal loaf that has nothing to do with liver or cheese. Of course, Hamburg's gift to the world is the **Hamburger Steak**—with a fried egg on top!

G Werbung für unsere Gaststätte

One of the ways to get customers to come to your restaurant is through advertising. Printed advertisements range from flyers distributed on car windshields to newspaper and magazine ads. Radio and television ads are generally more expensive and complicated than print ads.

Brauchbares

- Local newspaper, radio, and television advertisements
- Advertisements in German from newspapers or magazines
- Cassette recorder and/or video camera

Nützliche Vokabeln

„Licht! Kamera! Action!!“	*“Lights! Camera! Action!”*
die Annonce, -n/die Anzeige, -n	*advertisement, print ad*
die Filmmusik/der Soundtrack	*sound track*
[etwas] auf Tonband aufzeichnen	*to audiotape [something]*
die Geräuscheffekte	*sound effects*
der Regisseur/die Regisseurin	*director*
der Schauspieler/die Schauspielerin	*actor/actress*
schneiden	*to cut*
an der Kreuzung	*at the intersection of*
die Broschüre, -n/der Prospekt, -e	*brochure*
die Eröffnungsfeier, -n	*grand opening celebration*
das Flugblatt, ¨-er	*flyer*
gegenüber von	*across from, facing*
gelegen	*located*
das Sonderangebot, -e	*special offer*

Verknüpfungen

- ☑ Kunst
- ☑ Medien
- ☑ Musik
- ☑ Technik

Große Eröffnungsfeier am 3. September!

Gaststätte Schlaue Schüler
Kücknitzer Hauptstraße 31
Lübeck

Wir servieren ... die beste norddeutsche Küche.

Fischgerichte, Krabben, Muscheln, Fleisch und Geflügel.
Gegenüber vom Trave-Gymnasium, nahe Bus und Bahn

1. Schritt

Ein Flugblatt

Create a flyer in German announcing the opening of your restaurant. Include the name, location, and type of food served. Add directions to the restaurant, including a simple map.

2. Schritt

Eine Zeitungsanzeige

A. Read some restaurant ads from your local newspaper or Yellow Pages and from one of the German-language sources listed in the **Brauchbares** box. Choose one ad to discuss with your group, answering the following questions:

1. Was für Informationen stehen in der Anzeige?
2. Wie ist der Ton dieser Anzeige?
3. Mit welchen Adjektiven wird das Restaurant in der Anzeige beschrieben?
4. Welche Design-Elemente werden in der Anzeige verwendet?

B. Now write a brief, catchy newspaper advertisement in German for your restaurant, using the ads you have analyzed as guides.

Noch etwas dazu

Die Szene Live announcements need to be simple and concise, but also lively and, in the case of television, visually interesting.

A. Choose a favorite radio or television advertisement and describe it in German for your group, answering the following questions:

1. Welche Informationen werden im Werbespot gegeben?
2. Ist der Ton ruhig oder animiert?
3. Hört man Hintergrundmusik und Geräusche? Was ist der Effekt?
4. Was sieht man im Werbespot?
5. Wie viele Leute sieht oder hört man?

B. Write a script in German for your own radio or television ad publicizing your restaurant. Add background sounds and music. Consider interviewing restaurant patrons or staff members. Write! Produce! Direct! Star! If you can, record your radio ad on audiotape, or videotape your television spot.

H Einkaufen gehen

Before your restaurant's grand opening, you will need to order the food required to prepare your dishes.

Brauchbares

- Menu for your restaurant

1. Schritt Schreibt eine Einkaufsliste

Looking carefully at the menu for your restaurant, list in German the categories of foods you need to buy to prepare each menu item (fruits, vegetables, meats, and so on).

2. Schritt Lebensmittel einkaufen!

Which fresh food items will you purchase? List each item under the appropriate category, such as fruits, vegetables, and meats.

Obst	Gemüse	Fleisch
die Erdbeeren	die Tomaten	das Rindfleisch
die Äpfel	die Erbsen	das Lamm

3. Schritt Die Läden

Finally, next to or above each category on your list, write the type of store in which you will purchase the items. The food stores vocabulary in the Almanac will help you. In many German-speaking countries, people shop at smaller specialty shops, which often have fresher food or a better selection than supermarkets.

Verknüpfungen

☑ Gesundheit und Ernährung

Hast du das gewusst?

Traditionally, people in German-speaking countries shop daily in small neighborhood stores. Each shop specializes in a type of food, such as bread, pastries, meat and cold cuts, and dairy products. Small food stores (**Tante-Emma-Läden**) are quick sources of basics. Convenience, selection, and longer **Öffnungszeiten** (*store hours*) at **Supermärkte** have reduced the need for and number of smaller stores, but the small specialty stores are still doing well and provide high-quality food.

Noch etwas dazu

Lebensmittellieferung frei Haus. Sometimes restaurant owners order their groceries to be delivered, instead of going to the stores themselves.

A. From your shopping list, choose two stores you need to visit.

B. Working with a partner, take turns calling the shops you chose and ordering in German the groceries you need. Be specific about what you are ordering and include quantities in metric measures. (Consult the Almanac section of this book for information on weights and measures.) Give your name, business address, and phone number, and discuss prices. Be prepared to present your conversation to the class.

Noch etwas dazu

Unsere Spezialitäten sind lecker! As homework on the day before the grand opening of your restaurant, get together with your group and prepare the house specialty you will serve to your class the next day. Be ready to explain how the dish is prepared and served.

I Der Eröffnungstag!

After all your preparations, the big day is here. You are ready to open your restaurant. **Wir gratulieren!**

Brauchbares

- Your folder of materials created or gathered so far
- Tableware

Nützliche Vokabeln

Herzlich Willkommen!	*Welcome!*
Was gibt es auf der Speisekarte?	*What's on the menu?*
Was empfehlen Sie?	*What do you recommend?*
Ich würde vorschlagen, ___.	*I'd suggest ___.*
Wir möchten bestellen.	*We'd like to order.*
Was wünschen/möchten Sie?	*What would you like?*
Ich hätte gern ___./Ich möchte ___.	*I would like ___.*
Und zum Trinken?	*And to drink?*
Die Rechnung, bitte!	*The bill, please!*
das Trinkgeld, -er	*tip*

1. Schritt — Rollenverteilung für die Schauspieler

Working with your group and the group you interviewed for restaurant positions, choose roles to play in your restaurant. Remember to have some people play the role of customers!

2. Schritt Deckt die Tische!

Set up a dining table for your group (push desks together if your classroom does not have tables). Decorate your part of the classroom with any materials you have created or collected. When it is time to open for business, turn on the background music.

3. Schritt Macht die Türen auf!

Finally, the dining room is ready. The owners greet the customers, who come in chatting in German. The customers find seats and begin to discuss the menu. Servers come to the table to take orders and answer questions. The rest is up to you!

Hast du das gewusst?

You will usually find **Bedienung im Preis eingeschlossen** written on German menus. This means that when you get your bill (**die Rechnung**), the server's 15% gratuity has automatically been added to the bill. You only tip more if the service was particularly good—typically, you simply round off the bill to the next whole schilling, euro, and so on. In German-speaking countries, you never leave money for the bill and tip lying on the table and leave. The server personally takes your money or credit card and says **Auf Wiedersehen!**

The currency you use in restaurants will gradually change over the next few years. On January 1, 1999, a brand-new name appeared on the list of international currencies: the euro (**der Euro**, **-s**). Initially used only for electronic transactions, the euro is destined to replace national currencies in countries belonging to the European Union (**Europäische Union**). Paper bills and coins will be introduced on January 1, 2002, and will be accepted along with the local currency. By June 2002, all local currencies will be totally withdrawn. The new European Central Bank (**Europäische Zentralbank**), which, like the U.S. Federal Reserve, issues currency, has been centered in Frankfurt am Main, making Frankfurt central Europe's major financial center. Euros will be accepted everywhere except in those countries that are not EU member nations and countries that voted to retain their own currency (such as Great Britain).

German

Almanac

Table of Contents

Web Search Guide

Searching the World Wide Web

The **World Wide Web**[1] contains vast resources that would be hard to locate without **search tools** such as **search engines** and **Web guides.** These two tools allow you to search the Web for useful information by using **keywords** and phrases. You may have already done such searches in English. You will find that doing a search in German is most productive if you use German search engines, Web guides, and keywords.

Some of these words and phrases are provided in **Suchen wir im Web!** boxes in individual projects, but you may need to find others more closely related to your specific topic. Brainstorm helpful German keywords and phrases with other students before you begin your search. When you don't know a word or phrase in German, look in a dictionary or ask your teacher.

Begin your search by **clicking** on the **search button** in your **browser's toolbar.** This will open a **Web site** that offers you a variety of search tools. One of these will probably be automatically chosen for you, but you can change the choice by clicking on the names of other search engines or Web guides. Usually, if you scroll to the bottom of the page, you'll find a pop-up box or **links** that bring you to browsers in other languages. Choose German and click on the link or the **go button**. If the search tool you are using doesn't seem to have an option for German, scroll back up the page and try clicking on a different search tool.

Once you have found a German search tool, it's time to begin your search in earnest. There are two ways that you can do this. The first is to use a Web guide. Web guides select sites for you and list information in general categories with more specific subcategories. Using a Web guide is often the quickest and easiest way to conduct a search. Let's say you want to find descriptions of schools in several German-speaking countries. Try clicking on "travel," then "destinations," then a country where German is spoken, then a city. If you are sent to a city's Web site, you will probably find a listing of schools or a way to search for them. Since each Web guide organizes its data differently, **paths** to the same information may vary.

The second way of searching the Web, using either a Web guide or a search engine, is to enter a **search term** in a **text field** and then click on a word like "go," "begin," or "search." This kind of search is useful only when your search term is very specific. If you search for the keyword "school," for example, your

[1] Terms in bold are defined in the glossary on the next page.

search engine will retrieve all pages that have the term "school" in them. Some of these pages will certainly describe specific schools, but others may include a description of someone's education or even schools of fish! If your search term is more than one word, you must put quotation marks around the entire term so that the search tool treats it as a single search item. If you don't enclose it in quotation marks, the search engine will look for each of those words separately and you'll end up with a lot of useless information. For instance, typing *Job Lane School* without quotation marks in an English text field would retrieve *all* pages relating to jobs, lanes, or schools.

No matter which search tool you use, you will eventually end up with a results page that has links to different Web sites that might or might not contain the information you are looking for. Often there is a short summary of the contents of the site. Scan these summaries, and choose the sites that you think will be most useful. If the results don't fit on one page, click on the link "next" at the bottom of the page.

You can also do more sophisticated searches than those described here. Although each search tool works slightly differently, the basic techniques for using them are fairly consistent. You can learn how each search tool can help you do more effective searches by clicking on terms like "help" or "advanced search."

Make sure you evaluate any sites you find to determine whether they are factual and complete. One way is to check several sites on the same topic or to check the information in a reputable print source, such as an encyclopedia.

Glossary of Web Search Terms

ADDRESS See **URL.**

BEGIN or **GO BUTTON** Appears next to a **pulldown menu** or **search term** box on a page. Clicking on it initiates the next action.

BOOKMARK Used to save a **Web site** address you want to return to. Click and hold on the bookmark menu and then choose "add bookmark." The names of other addresses you have saved will also appear in this menu.

BROWSE The act of moving through the **WWW** by means of **links**.

BROWSER A software application that allows you to access the resources of the **WWW**. Netscape Navigator and Internet Explorer are examples of browsers.

CLICK The action of depressing a mouse button while the **pointer** is pointing at a specific object.

GO BUTTON See **begin button.**

HOMEPAGE A page that a user or organization has designated as the first page of its **Web site**.

HOT SPOTS Graphics or areas of graphics that allow you to **click** on a **link** that corresponds to the graphic.

INTERNET A vast, worldwide network of computers and related networks that are able to communicate with each other by means of common standards.

KEYWORD See **search term.**

LINK Words or graphics that allow you to move within a document or to another document on the **Internet**. Text links are often indicated by words that are highlighted in a different color and/or underlined. Graphic links are sometimes outlined in a contrasting color. Links can always be identified by the way your **pointer** changes as you pass over them. Also known as "hyperlink."

LOCATION BOX Contains the **URL** of the page that you are looking at. This is the information that you will need to note to locate a page again quickly, or you can **bookmark** it.

NAVIGATION Similar to **browsing,** but is usually more focused.

NET Short for **Internet.**

NET SEARCH BUTTON A button on the **toolbar** that accesses a variety of **search tools.**

PAGE Document on the **WWW**; also referred to as **Web page**.

PATH The route one follows to arrive at a list of **Web sites** when using a **Web guide**.

POINTER Associated with movement of your mouse. It changes shape for different functions that are defined by the software program you are using. Common functions are an arrow to indicate where you are on a screen, a hand to indicate a **link,** and an I-bar to indicate that you can enter text.

PULLDOWN MENU Shows the options associated with that menu. **Scrolling** to the desired option and releasing the mouse selects the option. The resulting action may occur automatically or you may need to click on a **go, begin,** or **start button.**

SCROLL The act of moving through an electronic document.

SCROLL BARS Bars at the edges of a document that allow you to move through the document.

SEARCH BUTTON Similar to the **begin button,** a button that initiates a search.

SEARCH ENGINE A program that works with your **browser** to find information on the **Web**.

SEARCH TERM The word or phrase you use to find specific content in a **search engine** or **Web catalog.**

SEARCH TOOL A **search engine** (such as Alta Vista) or **Web guide** (such as Yahoo!).

START BUTTON See **begin button.**

SURF See **browse.**

TOOLBAR Graphics and/or text at the top of a **browser** that allow you to initiate certain functions by clicking on the graphics or text.

TEXT FIELD The area in which you type in text on-screen. For example, the place you type in your **search term** in a **search engine**.

URL Short for Uniform Resource Locator, and sometimes known as an **address.** URLs are used for identifying all content on the **WWW**.

WEB Short for **World Wide Web.**

WEB CATALOG See **Web guide.**

WEB GUIDE A database of **Web pages** and other materials on the **Web.** These pages and materials are reviewed regularly for their usefulness and appropriateness to the subject heading used in the catalog.

WEB PAGE A document on the **WWW**, often containing text and graphics.

WEB SITE A collection of related **Web pages** in a single location connected by **links.**

WORLD WIDE WEB A part of the **Internet** that allows users to exchange information using text, graphics, sound, animation, and video.

WWW Short for **World Wide Web.**

German-Speaking Countries, Capitals, and Monetary Unit Chart

Country	Capital	Monetary Unit
Deutschland	Since 1990: Berlin	German mark
Europäische Union	——	euro
Fürstentum Liechtenstein	Vaduz	Swiss franc
Luxemburg[2]	Luxemburg	Luxemburg franc
Österreich	Vienna	Austrian schilling
die Schweiz	Bern	Swiss franc

To calculate the amount of foreign currency in dollars, simply multiply the dollar amount by the current exchange rate. For example, if \$1 = 6.2 Swiss francs, then \$20 = 124 Swiss francs (20 x 6.2).

die Schweiz

1 Franken = 100 Rappen

Österreich

1 Schilling = 100 Groschen

[2] Although **Lëtzebuergesch** or Luxembourgish is the national language of Luxembourg, both German and French are official languages and most people are bilingual, if not trilingual.

Deutschland
1 Mark = 100 Pfennig

Europäische Union
1 euro = 100 cents

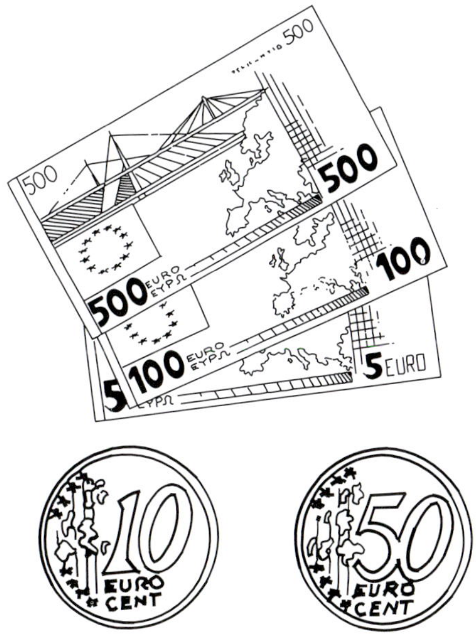

Euro notes symbolize Europe's architectural heritage, and do not represent any existing monument or specific country. Euro coins carry one common European face (like the 10 and 50 cents), and on the other side, each country has its own motif (see right). Any coin can be used in any EU country. For example, an Austrian citizen will be able to buy a soda in Spain using a coin carrying the imprint of the Brandenburg gate!

Deutschland
20 euro cents

Österreich
2 euros

Suchen wir im Web!

From a Web guide, type "exchange rates" in quotation marks in the Search Keyword box and click on Search to locate Web sites that provide daily rates of exchange of currencies throughout the world. Once the list of selected items comes up, review the descriptions and investigate sites that you think will have the exchange rate you require.

Clothing and Accessories

die (Sonnen)brille *(sun)glasses*
das (Strand)kleid *(sun)dress*
die Accessoires *accessories*
der Badeanzug *bathing suit*
die Bluse *blouse*
der Button-down-Kragen *button-down collar*
die Daunenjacke *down jacket*
der Gürtel *belt*
die Handtasche *handbag, purse*
das Hemd *shirt*
die Baggyhose *baggy jeans*
die Hose *pants*
der Hut *hat*
die Jacke *jacket*
die Krawatte *tie*
die Latzhose *overalls*
der Mantel *coat*
die Mütze *cap*
der Overall *jumpsuit*
das Polohemd *knit shirt, polo shirt*
der Pullover/der Pulli *pullover sweater*
das Top *tank top*
der Rock *skirt*
die Sandalen *sandals*
die Schuhe *shoes*
die Shorts (die kurze Hose) *shorts*

Expressions

Es ist sehr schick. *It's very stylish.*
Ja, es passt gut. *Yes, it fits well.*
Passt es? *Does it fit?*
Wie viel/Was kostet ___? *How much does ___ cost?*

die Socken *socks*
die Freizeitkleidung *casual clothing*
die Turnschuhe *sneakers*
der Rollkragen *turtleneck*
die Stiefel *boots*
das Sweatshirt mit Kapuze *hooded sweatshirt*
der Trainingsanzug *jogging suit*
das T-Shirt *T-shirt*

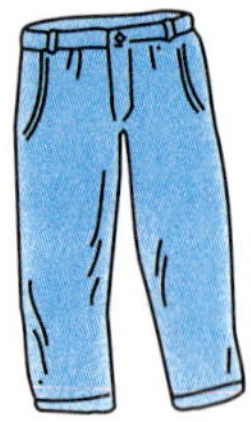

Clothing Descriptions

die Baumwolle *cotton*
bedruckt *print*
bunt *colorful*
der Cordsamt *corduroy*
geblümt *flowered*
gestreift *striped*
kariert *checked*
kurzärmelig *short-sleeved*
langärmelig *long-sleeved*
das Leder *leather*
die neueste Mode *the latest style*
schön *pretty*
die Seide *silk*
die Tupfen *polka-dot*
die Wolle *wool*

Size Conversion Chart[3]

Men's Suits

U.S	36	38	40	42	44	46
Europe	46	48	51	54	56	58

Men's Shirts

U.S.	14	14.5	15	15.5	16	16.5
Europe	36	37	38	39	40	41

[3] These are approximate conversions. There are variations among countries.

Women's Dresses, Coats, Blouses

U.S.	6	8	10	12	14	16
Europe	36	38	40	42	44	46

Women's Shoes

U.S.	6	6.5	7	7.5	8	8.5	9	9.5	10
Europe	37	38	38	39	39	40	40	41	41

Men's Shoes

U.S.	7.5	8	8.5	9	9.5	10	10.5	11	11.5	12
Europe	41	41	42	43	43	44	44	45	45	46

Clubs and Organizations

die Deutsch Arbeitsgemeinschaft (AG[4]) *German club*
die Foto AG *photography club*
die Französisch AG *French club*
die Latein AG *Latin club*
die Literaturzeitschrift *literary magazine*
die Mathe AG *math club*
AG für Naturwissenschaften *science club*

die Rhetorik AG *debate club*
der Schachverein *chess club*
die Schülervertretung *student government*
der Schiverein *ski club*
die Spanisch AG *Spanish club*
die Theater AG *drama club*

Colors

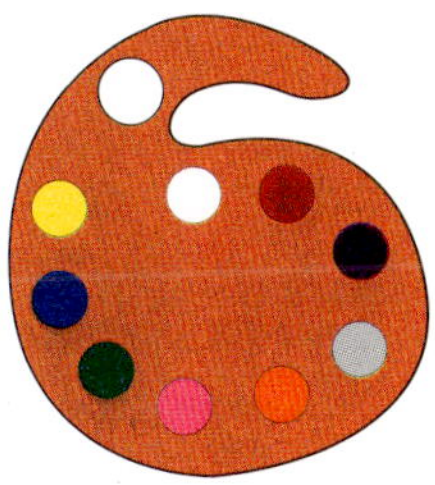

blau *blue*
braun *brown*
dunkelgrün *dark green*
ganz weiß *solid white*
gelb *yellow*
grau *gray*
hellblau *light blue*
kastanienbraun *maroon*
lila *purple*
marineblau *navy blue*
orange *orange*
rosa *pink*
rot *red*
schwarz *black*
silber *silver*
weiß *white*

Food and Nutrition

die Ananas *pineapple*
der Apfel *apple*
die Aprikose *apricot*
die Banane *banana*
die grünen Bohnen *green beans*
die Bratensoße *gravy*
das Brot *bread*
das Brötchen/die Semmel *roll*
das Ei (weich gekocht) *egg (soft-boiled)*
das Eis *ice cream*
die Erbsen *peas*
die Erdbeeren *strawberries*
der Fisch *fish*
das Fleisch *meat*

[4] AG = Arbeitsgemeinschaft. Clubs are called **AG's** in schools and **Vereine** outside of school.

die Frischwaren *perishable foods*
die Frucht/das Obst *fruit*
die Gefrierkost *frozen foods*
das Gemüse *vegetable*
die Grapefruit *grapefruit*
der Hamburger *hamburger*
das Hähnchen *chicken*
der Kaffee *coffee*
die Karotte *carrot*
die Kartoffel *potato*
der Käse *cheese*
die Kekse *cookies*
die Kirsche *cherry*
das Kohlenhydrat *carbohydrate*
der Kuchen *cake*
die Lasagne *lasagna*
die Marmelade *jam*
die Milch *milk*
das Mineral(ien) *mineral/minerals*
das Molkereiprodukt *dairy product*
das Öl *oil*
die Orange *orange*
der Pfirsich *peach*

die Pizza *pizza*
die Pommes frites *French fries*
das Popcorn *popcorn*
das Protein *protein*
der Reis *rice*
die Rosine *raisin*
der Saft *juice*
der Salat *salad*
das (Erdnussbutter und Marmelade) Sandwich *(peanut butter and jelly) sandwich*
der Schinken *ham*
das Schweineschmalz *lard*
die Spaghetti *spaghetti*
die Suppe *soup*
die Süßigkeiten *sweets*
der Tee *tea*
die Torte *pie*
vegetarisch *vegetarian*
das Vitamin *vitamin*
das Vollkornbrot *coarse, whole-grain bread*
die Weintraube *grape*
die Wurst *sausage, cold cuts*
der Zucker *sugar*

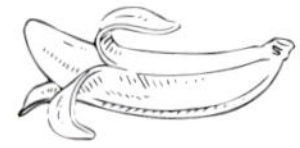

Expressions

durch(gebraten) *well done*
ganz wenig *very little, sparingly*
medium *medium*
englisch (gebraten) *rare*
Versuch weniger Fett zu essen. *Try to eat less fat.*
Versuch mehr Gemüse zu essen. *Try to eat more vegetables.*
Was würden Sie empfehlen? *What would you suggest?*

Gasthof zum Brunnen
Am Brunnenplatz 127, Bergwitz
Täglich geöffnet von 11 bis 21.30 Uhr

VORSPEISEN
Lachs auf Toast $6.95
Tagessuppe: Leberknödelsuppe $4.25
Gemischter Salatteller $6.50

HAUPTGERICHTE
Rheinischer Sauerbraten mit Spätzle $16.50
Schweinebraten mit Salzkartoffeln $15.95
Paniertes Wiener Schnitzel $12.75
Scampi in Kräuterbuttersoße $16.00
Halbes Hähnchen mit Bratkartoffeln $11.75

GETRÄNKE
Mineralwasser $1.75
Limonade $2.25
Kaffee, Tee $1.25

NACHSPEISE
Rote Grütze $4.75
Frische Erdbeertorte mit Schlagsahne $5.75

(Prices in US$) (Bedienung im Preis eingeschlossen)

Food Stores

die Bäckerei *bakery*
das Fischgeschäft *fish shop*
der Fleischer/der Metzger/der Schlachter[5] *butcher*
die Konditorei *pastry shop*
das Lebensmittelgeschäft *grocery store*
der Markt *market*
der Milchladen *dairy store*
der Verkäufer/die Verkäuferin *salesman/saleswoman*

[5] **Der Metzger:** in **Westmittel-** and **Süddeutschland**; **der Schlachter**: in **Norddeutschland**.

Expressions

Das macht [$]. *That's [$].*
ein Pfund ___ *a pound of ___*
Ich möchte bitte ein (Kilo)gramm ___. *I'd like a kilo(gram) of ___ please.*
Ich muss Botengänge/Besorgungen machen. *I need to run errands.*
Wie viel schulde ich Ihnen? *How much do I owe you?*

Furniture and Furnishings

die Möbel *(pl.) (furniture)*

der Bücherschrank *bookcase*
die Couch/das Sofa *couch*
das Doppelbett *double bed*
das Einzelbett *(twin) bed*
das Etagenbett *bunk bed*
der (Falt)stuhl *(folding) chair*
die Fußbank *footstool*
die Kommode *chest of drawers*
der Nachttisch *nightstand*
der Schaukelstuhl *rocking chair*
der Schreibtisch *desk*
der Sessel *armchair*
der Tisch *table*

die Einrichtungsgegenstände *(furnishings)*

die Beleuchtung *lighting*
die Bettdecke *comforter*
das Bild *picture*
der CD-Spieler *CD player*
der Fernseher *television*
gefliest *tiled (floor, walls)*
gestrichen *painted (wall, furniture)*
das Foto *photo*
die Jalousie *shade (Venetian blind)*
der Kassettenspieler *tape recorder*
das Kissen *pillow*
die (verstellbare) Lampe *(adjustable) lamp*
das Poster *poster*
das Radio *radio*
der Spiegel *mirror*
die Stereoanlage *stereo system*
streichen/malen *to paint*
die Tagesdecke *bedspread*
die Tapete *wallpaper*
das Telefon *telephone*
der Teppich *rug*
mit Teppichboden auslegen *to carpet*
der Vorhang *curtain*

Im Zimmer *(room)*

der Boden *floor*
die Decke *ceiling*
das Fenster *window*
der Schrank *closet*
die Tür *door*
die Wand *wall*

Expressions

Viel Spaß als Raumgestalter! *Have fun as interior decorators!*
Wir streichen ___ ___ an. *We're painting [the object] [color].*
Wir tapezieren die Wände. *We're wallpapering the walls.*

Holidays

die Fahne *flag*
die Feier *celebration*
die Feierlichkeiten *festivities*
feiern *to celebrate*
der Feiertag *legal holiday*
das Feuerwerk *fireworks*
gedenken *to commemorate*
historisch *historic*
die (National)hymne *(national) anthem*
militärisch *military*
die Musik *music*
der Nationalfeiertag *national holiday*
politisch *political*
religiös *religious*
das Symbol *symbol*
die Tradition *tradition*
der Umzug *parade*
die Zeremonie *ceremony*
zivil *civil*

Some Holidays

Chanukka *Hanukkah*
Mardi gras *Mardi Gras*
Neujahrstag *New Year's Day*
Ostern *Easter*
das Passahfest *Passover*
der Ramadan *Ramadan*
Tag der Arbeit *Labor Day*
Weihnachten *Christmas*

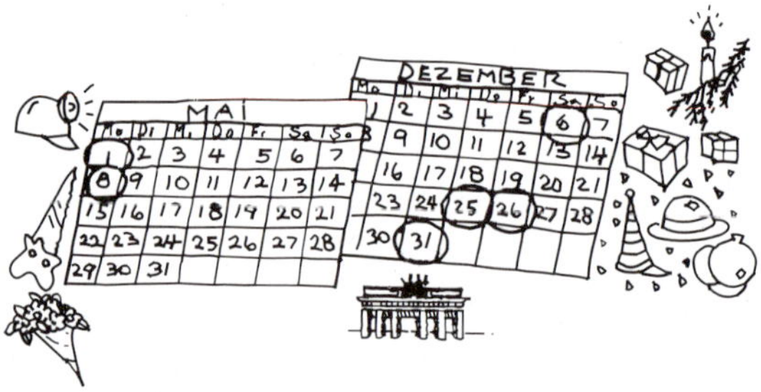

Musical Instruments

der Bass *bass*
die Blockflöte *recorder*
die Bratsche *viola*
das Cello *cello*
die Flöte *flute*
die Gitarre *guitar*
das Horn *horn*
die Klarinette *clarinet*
die Klaviatur *keyboard*
das Klavier *piano*

die Mundharmonika *harmonica*
die Oboe *oboe*
die Posaune *trombone*
das Saxophon *saxophone*
die Trommel *drum*
die Trompete *trumpet*
die Tuba *tuba*
die Violine *violin*
das Waldhorn *French horn*

Sports and Games

General Terms

der Athlet *athlete*
das Bandmaß *measuring tape*
gewinnen *to win*

der Gewinner *winner*
die Mannschaft *team*
messen *to measure*

mogeln/schummeln *to cheat*
Punkt machen *to score a point*
der Spielstand *score*
die Startlinie *starting line*
verlieren *to lose*
der Verlierer/die Verliererin *loser*
Wie steht es? *What's the score?*
das Ziel *finish line*

Sports

das Aerobic *aerobics*
der Baseball *baseball*
der Basketball *basketball*
das Eishockey *ice hockey*
das Fechten *fencing*
das Felsklettern *rock climbing*
der Football/der amerikanische Football *American football*
der Fußball *soccer*
Gewichte heben *to do weight lifting*
das Golf *golf*
die Gymnastik/das Turnen *gymnastics*
das Hockey *field hockey*
die Kampfsportarten *martial arts*
der Langlauf *cross-country skiing*
die Leichtathletik *track and field*
das Reiten *horseback riding*
das Ringen *wrestling*
das Rudern *rowing, crew*
das Schwimmen *swimming*
das Schilaufen *skiing*
das Wasserschilaufen *water-skiing*

Games

die Karten austeilen/mischen *deal/shuffle the cards*
das Spielbrett *game board*
der Spieler/die Spielerin *player*
die Spielkarten; das Kartenspiel *deck of cards; card game*
der Spielstein/die Spielfigur *playing piece*
die Stoppuhr; die Sanduhr *timer; hourglass*
der Würfel/die Würfel *die/dice*

Expressions

Auf die Plätze! *On your mark!*
Fertig! *Get set!*
Los! *Go!*
[Anne] ist jetzt dran/an der Reihe. *Now it's [Anne's] turn.*
Du bist dran/an der Reihe. *It's your turn.*
Geh zum/zur ___. *Go to ___.*
Geh ___ Feld(er) vorwärts./Rücke ___ Plätze vorwärts. *Move ahead ___ space(s).*
Geh ___ Feld(er)/Plätze zurück. *Go back ___ spaces.*
Heb/Nimm eine Karte ab. *Pick up/draw a card.*
Ich bin dran/an der Reihe. *It's my turn.*
Ich brauche zwei Karten. *I need two cards.*
Setz deine Spielfigur an den Start. *Put your piece on the starting space.*
Wenn du auf ___ landest, geh zum/zur ___. *If you land on ___, go to ___.*
Wer ist dran/an der Reihe? *Whose turn is it?*
Wie viele Karten brauchst du? *How many cards do you need?*
Wollen wir ein Spiel spielen? *How about playing a game?*
Würfel! *Roll the dice!*
Zähle! *Count!*

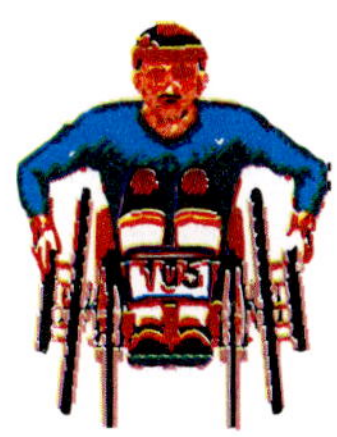

Subjects and Courses

Algebra *algebra*
amerikanische Geschichte *American history*
Biologie *biology*
Chemie *chemistry*
Deutsch *German*
Englisch *English*
Französisch *French*
Geometrie *geometry*
Hauswirtschaft *home economics*
Informatik *computer science*
Japanisch *Japanese*
Kapelle/Band *band*
Kommunikationswissenschaft *communications*
Kunst *art*
Latein *Latin*
Mathematik (Mathe) *mathematics (math)*
Musik *music*
Orchester *orchestra*
Philosophie *philosophy*

Physik *physics*
Psychologie *psychology*
Publizistik/Journalismus *journalism*
Analysis *calculus*
Russisch *Russian*
Singen/Chor *singing/chorus*
Sozialkunde *social studies*
Soziologie *sociology*
Spanisch *Spanish*
Sport/Turnen *physical education*
Tanzen *dance*
Theater *theater/acting*
Wirtschaftskunde *economics*
Weltgeschichte *world history*
Werken *shop*
Betriebswirtschaft *business*
Wissenschaft *science*
(technisches) Zeichnen *(technical) drawing*

Weather

Wie ist das Wetter? *How's the weather?*

Schönes Wetter *(nice weather)*

die Aufheiterungen *sunny spells*
Das Wetter ist schön. *The weather is nice.*
Es ist sonnig. *It's sunny.*
klar *clear*
sonnig *sunny*
wolkenlos *cloudless*

Die Wolken *(clouds)*

bedeckt *overcast*
bewölkt/wolkig *cloudy*
Es ist bewölkt/wolkig. *It's cloudy.*
der Nebel/neblig *fog/foggy*
stark bewölkt *very cloudy*

Der Regen *(rain)*

Es gießt (in Strömen). *It's pouring.*
Es nieselt. *It's drizzling.*
Es schüttet wie aus Eimern. *It's raining cats and dogs ("buckets").*
der Regenguss *downpour*
der Regentag *rainy day*
der Schauer *shower (of rain)*
der Sprühregen, der Nieselregen *drizzle*
die Überschwämmung, das Hochwasser *flood*

Schlechtes Wetter *(bad weather)*

der Blitz *lightning*
die Brise *breeze*
Das Wetter ist schlecht. *The weather is bad.*
der Donner *thunder*
Es hagelt. *It's hailing.*
Es ist nasskalt. *It's damp and cold.*
Es ist schwül. *It's humid.*
Es ist windig. *It's windy.*
das Gewitter *thunderstorm*
der Hagel *hail*
der Hurrikan *hurricane*
die Hurrikan-/die Tornado-/die Wirbelsturmwarnung *hurricane, tornado warning*
der Niederschlag *precipitation*
trüb *murky*
der Wind *wind*
der Wirbelsturm, der Tornado *tornado*

Kaltes Wetter *(cold weather)*

eingeschneit sein *to be snowed in*
eisig *icy*
Es schneit. *It's snowing.*
der Frost *frost*
der Schnee *snow*
der Schneefall *snowfall*
der Schneeregen *sleet*
der Schneesturm *snowstorm*

Temperature: Fahrenheit and Celsius Conversion

As you change temperatures from one system to another, notice that you are using opposite math operations.

To convert Fahrenheit to **Celsius**, subtract 32 from the Fahrenheit temperature and divide by 1.8.

To convert Celsius to **Fahrenheit**, multiply the Celsius temperature by 1.8 and add 32.

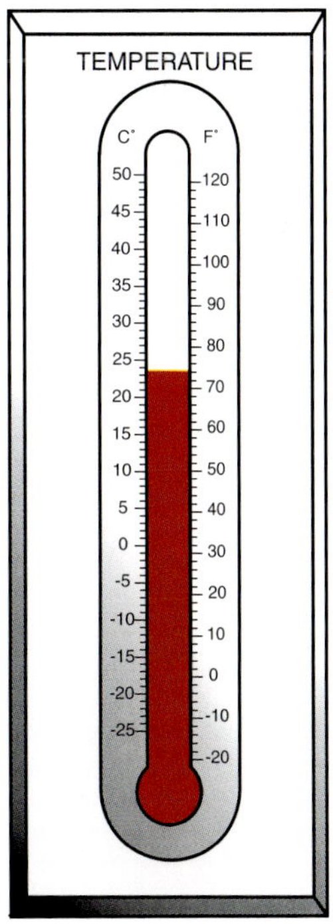

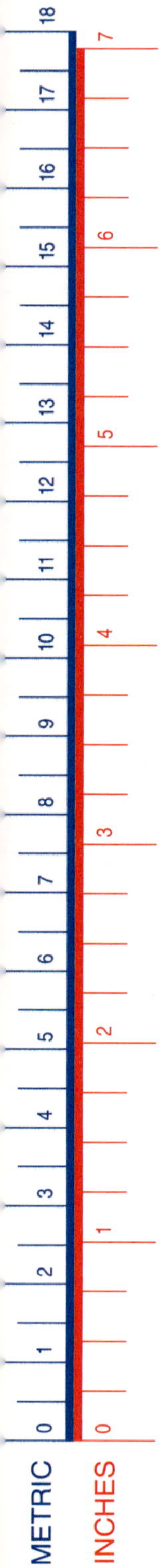

Weights and Measures

Weight

Metric	American/Standard
1 gram	0.03 ounce
1 kilogram (kilo)	2.2 pounds
28 grams	1 ounce
0.45 kilogram	1 pound
900 kilograms	2,000 pounds (1 ton)

Liquid Measure

Metric	American/Standard
1 liter	1.06 quarts
0.47 liter	1 pint
0.95 liter	1 quart
3.8 liters	1 gallon

Distance

Metric	American/Standard
1 meter	39.5 inches (1.1 yards)
1 kilometer	0.62 mile
2.54 centimeters	1 inch
0.3 meter	1 foot
0.9 meter	1 yard
1.6 kilometers	1 mile

Conversion

Multiply **miles** by 1.61 to get **kilometers**
Multiply **kilometers** by 0.62 to get **miles**

Multiply **inches** by 2.54 to get **centimeters**
Multiply **centimeters** by 0.39 to get **inches**

Multiply **feet** by 0.30 to get **meters**
Multiply **meters** by 3.48 to get **feet**

Multiply **yards** by 0.91 to get **meters**
Multiply **meters** by 1.09 to get **yards**

German Equivalents

der Fuß *foot*
das Gramm *gram*
das Kilogramm *kilogram*
der Kilometer *kilometer*
der Liter *liter*
die Meile *mile*
der Meter *meter*
das Pfund *pound*
die Pinte *pint*
das Quart *quart*
die Tonne *ton*
die Unze *ounce*
das Yard *yard*
der Zentimeter *centimeter*
der Zoll *inch*

Writing Letters

German speakers usually include the city from where they are writing in front of the date, even in a personal letter.

For the date, use **den** + cardinal number followed by a period + month + year.

In writing to a friend, **Liebe(r)** (*Dear*) is the most common greeting. Between two young people, **Hallo** (*Hi*) is also fine. In formal letters, **Sehr geehrte(r)** is the standard salutation, followed by **Herr** or **Frau** (*Mr. or Mrs./Ms.*). Don't forget to make it agree: **geehrter Herr** or **geehrte Frau**.

Chicago, den 21. September 2002

Lieber Martin,

ich heiße Tom. Ich bin 14 Jahre alt. Ich komme aus Chicago, Illinois. Ich habe zwei Brüder und einen Hund (wir sind alle auf dem Foto). Ich spiele gern Tennis, lese gern und gehe gern schwimmen. Bis bald!

Viele Grüße

Tom

Since the first line of a German letter is considered the same sentence as the salutation, it is not capitalized.

As a sign-off for this letter, **Viele Grüße** (*Best Wishes*) is a good choice. Use **Alles Liebe**, **Viele liebe Grüße**, or **Deine(e)** in most personal letters (*All my love, Lots of love, Yours*) or **Herzliche Grüße** (*Best wishes*) for someone close to you.

XXX XXXXX
XXXX XXXXXXX XXXX
XXXX, XX
U.S.A

An
Herrn Martin Schmidt
Mommsengasse 6/15
A-5020 Salzburg
AUSTRIA

In an international letter, be sure to include your country (U.S.A., Canada) below the city and state or province.

The postal code goes before the city. The country name is usually in all caps.

Street names, such as **Engelstraße** or **Rennweg**, precede the house or apartment number. Note that *street* is often shortened: **Engelstraße** can be written as **Engelstr.**

The titles **Herrn** (accusative after **An**) or **Frau** are generally included in formal correspondence and precede the person's name. **Fräulein** is falling out of use. **An** is placed on the line above.

Notes

Notes